A HISTORY OF
FORT SUMTER

A HISTORY OF

FORT SUMTER

BUILDING A CIVIL WAR LANDMARK

M. PATRICK HENDRIX

THE
History
PRESS

Published by The History Press
Charleston, SC 29403
www.historypress.net

All images are courtesy of the Library of Congress.

First published 2014

Manufactured in the United States

ISBN 978.1.62619.470.0

Library of Congress CIP data applied for.

CONTENTS

ACKNOWLEDGEMENTS

I would first like to like to thank Toni Hendrix and Judy Corbett for their contributions on this project. Their editing was a godsend. Danna Gosney and Eric Poplin also helped edit and gave many useful insights. Additionally, I would like to express my gratitude to the staffs at The History Press, Fort Moultrie, the Charleston Public Library, The Citadel Military College and the South Caroliniana Library. Finally, I would like to thank Steven Smith, an archaeologist with the South Carolina Institute of Archaeology and Anthropology who gave my last book a particularly nasty review. After an initial moment of anger where I might've referred to Dr. Smith as a vicious skunk or much worse, I figured any publicity was better than no publicity. I was mistaken. Turns out only the terminally dull or mentally deranged would read something called *The Public Historian*. Alas, no bump in sales. I do, however, thank Steven for his insights and wanted to mention him here so that his name might appear in a publication that human beings actually read. (This is, of course, all in good fun.)

Hope you enjoy it. If you don't, I'm putting you in the acknowledgements of my next book.

PH

1
CONCEPTION

It was an uneasy night in August 1814. Enduring the hottest summer anyone could remember and plagued by the malarial swamps surrounding the city, Washington's residents awoke on August 24 to hear that thousands of battle-hardened veterans of the Napoleonic Wars were marching from the Chesapeake Bay and their arrival was imminent. With the capital's defenses in hopeless disrepair, Washington's prospects looked grim, and half the city fled in advance of the British Expeditionary Force.

By midafternoon on the twenty-fourth, 4,500 British troops were just miles from the city when a combined force of U.S. Army regulars, marines and militia tried one final stand at the town of Bladensburg, Maryland. President James Madison and most of his cabinet were in attendance as the Americans opened the engagement with artillery and small arms fire. The Americans were soon thrown back by the Forty-fourth Regiment of Foot, and the American lines soon crumbled and fell away. Though Commodore Joshua Barney's flotilla men and Captain Samuel Miller's marines tried to rally, by four o'clock, the Americans were finished.

As darkness approached, General Robert Ross's Expeditionary Force reconnoitered at the outskirts of Washington. After a brief pause to organize his forces, Ross sent word to the city's residents to surrender. When his terms were answered with musket fire from a nearby window, this "breach of the law of nations, roused the indignation of every individual, from the General himself down to the private soldier." All those found where the shots were fired were executed, and the house was torched. As the sun edged below the

The White House after its destruction by the British during the War of 1812.

horizon, British forces marched to Capitol Hill and proceeded to destroy "everything in the most distant degree connected with government." British soldier George Robert Gleig reported that his compatriots arrived to see that "the sky was brilliantly illuminated." He recalled:

The blazing of houses, ships, and stores, the report of exploding magazines, and the crash of falling roofs informed them, as they proceeded, of what was going forward. You can conceive nothing finer than the sight which met them as they drew near to the town…a dark red light was thrown upon the road, sufficient to permit each man to view distinctly his comrade's face.

As the British troops delighted in burning Washington's public buildings, another detachment was sent to "Mr. Madison's house," where they found the White House dinner table prepared for forty guests, though "lately and precipitately abandoned." After sitting down to enjoy wine and a meal served on the president's finest plate, "they finished by setting fire to the house which had so liberally entertained them."[1]

With Washington in ruins and the country heading toward insolvency, the United States was undoubtedly taking a beating. But where the Republic failed on the battlefield, it would triumph in a sort of strategic default. The British could burn Washington and "chastise the savages," but outright victory over the Americans could only be accomplished by mobilizing tens of thousands of Napoleonic Wars veterans. While the British press called for complete "submission," after calculating the logistical difficulties and political risks, British policymakers decided that the strategic accounting didn't add up.[2]

Looking to end the war, both sides met in Belgium and signed the Treaty of Ghent on December 24, 1814. Recognizing the United States as an equal of sorts, Great Britain relinquished claim to the Northwest Territory and accepted most of the American demands. Adding insult to injury, or perhaps vice versa, on January 8, 1815, Major General Andrew Jackson's combined force of American Regulars, Choctaws, frontiersmen, African American freemen, marines and sailors routed eight thousand British Expeditionary troops as they marched on New Orleans. In under an hour, the Americans turned the British columns into a bloody wreck, killed commanding officer Major General Sir Edward Pakenham—brother-in-law to the Duke of Wellington—and forced a British officer to surrender to a private of the Seventh Infantry as the American troops laughed. Jackson's dramatic victory not only avenged the burning of Washington but also prophesied a new empire that would, as one contemporary put it, "give quiet to the world."[3]

With the War of 1812 over, the country faced no imminent security threats. But soon, the French and British would get back to killing someone, and it was best to plan to plan for that eventuality. England was determined to maintain a powerful military presence in the Western Hemisphere, making it inevitable that the two countries' imperial ambitions would create new conflict. For their part, the French proved capable of trouncing all comers save the Russian winter, and their endless squabbles with the British always threatened to drag the United States into war. Even the Spanish Empire, then in precipitous decline, still endangered not only the Republic's "security, tranquility, and commerce" but also, as Thomas Jefferson warned, its very "destiny" to "give the law to our hemisphere." Senator Henry Clay cautioned that unless Americans wanted to "abandon the Ocean; surrender all your commerce; give up all your prosperity," it would be necessary to prepare for "foreign collision."[4]

Speaking to the danger, President Madison went to Congress on December 5, 1815, and declared:

> *The character of the times particularly inculcates the lesson that, whether to prevent or repel danger, we ought not to be unprepared for it. This consideration will sufficiently recommend to Congress a liberal provision for the immediate extension and gradual completion of the works of defense, both fixed and floating, on our maritime frontier.*[5]

Late in 1816, President Madison instructed Secretary of War George Graham to form a special board of officers to create a "permanent" and "comprehensive plan" of coastal defense. The War Department enlisted the help of Simon Bernard, a French military engineer who previously served as head of the French topographical bureau and brigadier general and aide-de-camp to Napoleon. Recommended by the Marquis de Lafayette, a hero of the American Revolution—and in need of new job after the Grande Army was routed at Waterloo—Bernard was given a brevet commission in the same grade and served as the president of the board of engineers. The "Bernard Board" consisted of one U.S. Navy engineer and two U.S. Army engineers, including brevet Lieutenant Colonel Joseph G. Totten. Despite Bernard's prominence in the early years, before the board finished its work, Totten had become one the world's foremost experts on seacoast fortifications and America's greatest military engineer.

Though the board focused on fortifications, the original plan was far more comprehensive, including "several interrelated elements—a navy, fortifications, avenues of communication in the interior, and a regular army and well-organized militia." Traveling the American coastline, the board consulted with local military planners and engineers to devise an integrated fortification system, determining the relative importance of each site and designing fortifications based on the best planning and construction standards of the early nineteenth century.

Five years after its formation, the board recommended that the navy take primary responsibility for coastal defense. Selected fortification sites were augmented by nearby naval bases, repair yards and anchorages to protect vital commercial seaports. Military planners knew Congress loathed spending money on defense during peacetime, so only eighteen defensive works were considered "urgent" in 1821. An additional thirty-two sites were recommended as possibilities for the future.[6]

Since military planners were most concerned with fortifying new territories in Florida and Louisiana, Charleston Harbor was neglected in the first congressional appropriation for the Third System. However, the city was an important commercial port, and consequently, in 1826, the board of engineers began to survey the Charleston Harbor and discovered a shallow shoal opposite Fort Moultrie that to that point had been a navigation hazard submerged at high tide. The engineering board felt if the sandbar were built up to be a man-made island, the defense of Charleston's Harbor "may be considered as an easy simple problem."

Though forts existed in Charleston, the guns located at Fort Moultrie on Sullivan's Island could not reach a ship hugging the ship channel's southern edge. Fort Johnson and Castle Pinckney could add fire, yet engineers thought them insufficient to command the channel, even when working in unison. What they needed was a way to create an interlocking field of fire, and that could only be accomplished by building another fort at the harbor's center.

In 1827, Secretary of War John C. Calhoun, a South Carolina native, a soon-to-be powerful proponent of nullification and an implacable enemy of the Federal government, approved the construction of a new fort in Charleston Harbor. It was eventually named in honor of Revolutionary War hero Brigadier General Thomas "the Gamecock" Sumter. Plans were drawn up, and in 1828, Congress made the first appropriation for building the fort. Fort Sumter would be "a pentagonal, three-tiered, masonry fort with truncated angles that was to be built on the shallow shoal extending from James Island."[7]

Engineers at Fort Sumter decided to use masonry not only because it was resistant to erosion but also because using brick allowed engineers to include casemate emplacements. Built into a wall or rampart, the casemate is a vaulted chamber for gun emplacements with openings known as embrasures. The casemates allowed engineers to maximize the number of guns at the fortification.

There was one problem with the use of brick at Fort Sumter. Since Bamburgh Castle succumbed to a sustained artillery barrage during the War of the Roses in 1464, military planners knew that vertical masonry walls could be battered down by concentrated cannon fire. Therefore, building the fort with high walls of brick was counterintuitive; but when the military planners were conceptualizing the fort, it was assumed that any incoming fire would come from light cannon fired from the gun ports of a boat. If the ordnance coming from enemy ships lacked the accuracy to hit the same spot repeatedly, then individual projectiles, which lacked the destructive power of land-based guns, would be unable to breach the walls. Experiments by Joseph Totten also proved to military planners that masonry could withstand solid cannon shot fired at close range.

Standing on a sandbar that would slip beneath an incoming tide, Lieutenant Henry Brewerton, supervisory engineer for Fort Sumter's construction, knew he faced a daunting task. The shoal shifted and reformed after storms, rendering it necessary to build a substantial foundation to stabilize the spot. Brewerton had to secure the materials necessary to build such a foundation and looked in New York and New England for quarries capable of providing "30,000 tons of stone, in irregular masses, weighing between 50 and 500 pounds." In September 1829, Brewerton accepted a proposal for 30,000 tons of stones at $2.45 per ton from Ralph Berkley in New York, provided that they were delivered on time and of a suitable quality, size and weight.

After the contractor managed to deliver only one thousand tons in a year, Brewerton instructed his chief engineer, Brigadier General Charles Gratiot, to cancel the contract. Another deal was secured with a quarry in Baintree, Massachusetts, for stone at $2.11 a ton. The plan was to create a semicircle of rock called a "mole." The open spot in the rocks would allow ships to enter the site at high tide to drop cargo on the shoal without being pounded by wind and waves. By 1834, the mole was completed, and Brigadier General Charles Gratiot reported to the board of engineers that fifty thousand tons of rough granite, stretchers and cut stone (for cisterns) had been delivered.[8]

THE LAVAL CLAIM AND THE NULLIFICATION CRISIS

By November 3, 1834, the Federal government had spent about $200,000 constructing Fort Sumter, and the foundation of the fort was taking shape. All seemed to be proceeding as planned when, in the same month, Brewerton received a letter from local resident Major William Laval that read:

> *Sirs: You are hereby notified that I have taken out, from under the seal of the State, a grant of all those shoals opposite and below Fort Johnson, on one of which the new work called Fort Sumter, is now erecting. You will consider this as notice of my right to the same; the grant is recorded in the*

office of the secretary of state of this State, and can be seen by reference to the records of that office. W. Laval.

The claim was sent to the "Engineer Superintending" in Charleston Harbor, Lieutenant T.S. Brown, who was away from the fort at the time. The letter was received by Dr. Robert Lebby, a civilian doctor under contract to provide for the medical needs of those working on the site's construction, and then forwarded to Brigadier General Gratiot.

By November 19, 1834, the Army Corps of Engineers had reviewed the claim and found that the 870-acre "plantation" was eight to ten feet below water.[9] No doubt, the engineers knew what Laval's claim was about—South Carolina's doctrine of nullification, which held that states could defy Federal actions and "internal improvements" by declaring them invalid or simply ignoring them. For Sandlappers, the clearest example of the metastasizing power of the Federal government was under construction at the mouth of the Charleston Harbor. By the early 1830s, Governor Robert Y. Hayne was searching for a way to stop the construction of Fort Sumter and began to rally the state for a potential showdown with the Federal government. In a message to the South Carolina legislature in 1833, Hayne warned about the "usurpation of the Federal Government" and talked openly about a separate "Confederation of states." He then informed the legislature that he was appointing Major William Laval, the very man who would lay claim to Fort Sumter, as comptroller general for the state.

Born in Charleston on May 27, 1788, Major Laval was described by one contemporary as "six feet high, very erect in person" with a "very striking and military appearance." He began his military career in October 1808 as an ensign stationed in Charleston Harbor at Forts Moultrie and Johnson. Serving as first lieutenant and later captain in the Creek Wars—leaving the fight only briefly to return home to participate in that most Charleston of pastimes, dueling—Laval was wounded at the siege of Pensacola, an injury that caused to him walk on crutches the remainder of his life.[10]

Following military service, Laval returned to Charleston as secretary of state of South Carolina and sheriff of Charleston and eventually as assistant treasurer of the United States under President James Polk and treasurer of the state of South Carolina. But it was Major Laval's brief stint as an officer in the Customs House that led him into the politics of nullification. When Laval used his position to enforce a South Carolina law to invalidate the tariffs of 1828 and 1832 and prevented Federal officials from collecting the tariffs, he was removed, as Governor Hayne put it, "from a lucrative position at the Customs House as punishment for his loyalty to his native state." Even his "services and suffering…under the eye of General Jackson" during the War of 1812 had proven insufficient "to shield him from that ruthless spirit of prescription which serves to consider fidelity to the State as incompatible with the duty of the Union."[11] For this loyalty, Laval was rewarded with the comptroller general position. It was also in this position that he could twist the construction of Fort Sumter into legal knots while South Carolina argued over the legitimacy of the Land Frontier and Seacoast Program.[12]

Although work ground to a halt in Charleston Harbor, tensions in South Carolina continued to increase. The pressure built for a decade as South Carolina faced a series of shocks that radicalized a state not known for its moderation. The first occurred in the spring of 1819, when cotton prices collapsed as overproduction pushed prices sharply lower. Worse still for South Carolina, many of the state's planters were picking up and moving west, leaving behind exhausted fields and gangs of slaves who could not be profitably put to work. Not only did cotton prices drop in South Carolina, but Charleston also lost enormous revenues as Mobile and New Orleans emerged as the South's most important ports. By 1828, the chamber of commerce reported that the city "has for several years past retrograded… Her land estate has within eight years depreciated in value one half. Industry and business talent…have sought employment elsewhere. Many of her houses are tenantless and the grass grows uninterrupted in some of her chief business streets."[13]

The migration of South Carolina's sons and daughters to the fertile soils of Alabama and beyond was worsened by the fact that the rest of the country was quickly gaining in population, a demographic trend that would surely erode the region's political clout. As fiery South Carolina partisan Robert Barnwell Rhett lamented, "Every census has added to the power of the non-slaveholding states and diminished that of the South." More immediately, the 1820 census showed that for the first time since the American Revolution, South Carolina had a black majority. In Charleston, 58 percent of the population was black, a percentage that increased yearly.[14]

To South Carolina's elite, economic depression, slave insurrection, abolitionist propaganda and the Federal government were all part of a conspiracy to destroy the South and its domestic institutions. Governor Bennett thought the state was heading toward disunion as early as 1823, writing to Thomas Jefferson: "I fear nothing so much as the Effects of the persecuting Spirit that is abroad in this Place [Charleston]. Should it spread thro', the State & produce a systematic Policy founded on the ridiculous but prevalent

In 1827, Secretary of War John C. Calhoun, a South Carolina native and implacable enemy of the Federal government, approved the construction of a new fort in Charleston Harbor.

Notion—that it is a struggle for Life or Death, there are no Excesses that we may not look for—whatever be their Effect upon the Union."[15] South Carolina was edging toward outright secession when, in April 1830, President Jackson offered a toast of "Our Federal Union—It must be preserved." His own vice president, South Carolinian John C. Calhoun, responded defiantly, "The Union—next to our liberty most dear; may we all remember that it can only be preserved by respecting the rights of the states and distributing equally the benefits and burden of the Union." The insult only added to the deepening animosity between the men that had begun when the president discovered that Calhoun had recommended that Jackson be court-martialed during the War of 1812. When Calhoun wrote a nine-thousand-word reply to the president to vindicate his position, Jackson tersely replied, "Et tu, Brute?" The Federal government and the state of South Carolina, led respectively by the president and vice president, were on a collision course.[16]

In the election of 1832, the nullifiers were swept into power by the narrowest of margins in one of the most toxic and corrupt elections in South Carolina history, certainly no small accomplishment in the Palmetto State. Despite the close election, in November 1832, the South Carolina legislature approved Calhoun's Ordnance of Nullification, which invalidated the tariffs of 1828 and 1832 and ordered state officials to stop collecting duties at South Carolina's ports. Jackson was warned that if the national government forced tax collection, South Carolina would leave the Union.

With the situation escalating, President Jackson issued a proclamation to bring South Carolina back from the brink:

Fellow citizens of my native State! let me not only admonish you, as the first Magistrate of our common country, not to incur the penalty of its laws, but use the influence that a Father would over his children whom he saw rushing to certain ruin…You are free members of a flourishing and happy union. There is not settled design to oppress you.—You have indeed felt the unequal operation of the laws which may have been unwisely, not constitutionally passed; but that inequality must necessarily be removed.

Though he sympathized with the unfairness of the tariff act, the president said that the "laws of the United States must be executed" and warned if South Carolina's "object is disunion…be not deceived by names: disunion, by armed force, is TREASON."[17]

The dictates of honor necessitated a firm response, and South Carolina promised to meet the president's challenge militarily. Jackson responded by sending naval reinforcements, three divisions of artillery and five thousand muskets to Castle Pinckney and demanding the commander of the harbor forts to hold them at all costs. "We must be prepared to act with promptness and crush the monster in its cradle before it matures to manhood," wrote Jackson to his secretary of war. The average soldier would not suffer alone. Jackson leveled his threat directly at South Carolina's political leaders, saying, "The moment I am prepared with proof I will direct prosecution for treason to be instituted against the leaders, and if they are surrounded with 12,000 bayonets our marshal shall be aided by 24,000 and arrest them in the midst thereof."[18]

With both sides retrenching, President Jackson relied on intelligence from Joel Roberts Poinsett, member of the United States House of Representatives and native a South Carolinian who had once served as a special agent to Chile and Argentina. Though Poinsett warned Jackson that the nullifiers were hoping the Federal government would "commit some act of violence, which will enlist the sympathies of the bordering states," the president remained undaunted. He told Poinsett he would "march 200,000 men in forty days to quell any and every insurrection or rebellion that might arise to threaten our glorious confederacy and Union, upon which our liberty, prosperity, and happiness rest."[19]

The state remained defiant. Calhoun resigned as vice president and was appointed senator. From the floor of the Senate chamber, he declared that Charleston's harbor forts were not there to protect the city but to "keep the people themselves in awe and subjection…the first instance in our history which the arms of the Republic were directed against her citizens."

Meanwhile in South Carolina, the General Assembly chose arch-secessionist Robert Y. Hayne as governor. The new governor promptly selected a new military aide de camp, tasked him with raising volunteer companies and ordered the formation of "mounted minute men" who could deploy to any area of the state threatened by Federal troops. The president was informed that South Carolina was preparing for war and "drill and exercise their men without intermission."[20]

Edging toward disunion and war, South Carolina looked to its neighbors for relief. This was a dangerous situation for Jackson. If he could keep South Carolina isolated, the situation could be contained. This strategy was complicated by the fact that the protective tariff was loathed by all southern states and powerful factions throughout the region wanted to cast their lots with South Carolina. Among the most vocal was Virginia's governor John Floyd, who stated if President Jackson used force, "I will oppose him with a military force. I nor my country will be enslaved without a struggle." Never one to let a threat go unanswered, Jackson blithely responded, "If the governor of Virginia should have the folly to attempt to prevent the militia from marching through his state to put the faction in South Carolina down…I would arrest him at the head of his troops."[21] Floyd promptly dropped the matter.

The rest of the South soon followed Floyd's example. Georgia called South Carolina's actions "reckless," while a Tennessean told the president that he would collect enough men "to stand in the Saluda Mountains and piss enough…to float the whole nullifying crew of South Carolina into the Atlantic Ocean." More ominously, Jackson said he would "hang every leader…of

When South Carolina promised to meet the president's challenge militarily, Andrew Jackson responded by sending naval reinforcements, three divisions of artillery and five thousand muskets to Castle Pinckney.

that infatuated people…by martial law, irrespective of his name, or political or social position." Considering the president was a man that mercilessly beat would-be assassins, committed acts of genocide against the Cherokee Indians and walked around with a bullet in his chest from one of his many duels, the leaders of South Carolina knew Old Hickory wasn't a man to take his word lightly. If Andy Jackson promised a hangman's noose, it was a damn good bet he meant it.[22]

All the talk came to naught. Realizing it could not nullify the U.S. Army or get any other southern state to follow it over the cliff, South Carolina soon found common ground with President Jackson. A compromise tariff was drafted and passed in Congress in 1834. Soon things deescalated, and the South Carolina legislature was looking for a resolution with the Federal government over Fort Sumter. Since Laval's claim, South Carolina's committee on Federal relations had challenged the Federal government's authority for a project in Charleston Harbor. On December 31, 1836, the committee relented and ceded to the United States, "all the right, title and claim of South Carolina to the site of Fort Sumter and the requisite quantity of adjacent territory…Also resolved: That the State shall extinguish the claim, if any valid claim there be, of any individuals under the authority of this State, to the land hereby ceded." If it were found that the claim was legitimate—and they all knew it wasn't—Generals Hamilton and Hayne, along with James L. Pringle, Thomas Bennett and Ker Boyce, were to serve as commissioners on behalf of the state to appraise the value of the property and pay off Laval.[23]

On December 20, 1837, South Carolina state attorney Jacob Warly invalidated Laval's claim, but from his seat in the U.S. Senate, the man who once "perfected and matured" the Federal system of fortifications, John C. Calhoun, looked for every opportunity to kill the program. First, Calhoun argued that the government could not justify the "extravagant expenditure," given that Congress would need to pay garrisons to man the fortifications. Besides, the U.S. Navy needed the Federal dollars. Next, he argued that "far from being defenceless, as far as fortifications are concerned, the country, with some exceptions, is in a state of admirable defence." Furthermore, there was "never a time when there was so little use in expending money on new fortifications." All difficulties were "happily settled" with France, and the willingness of the British to "settle our foolish and wicked quarrel with France, plainly showed her friendly intentions towards this country, and her strong desire to maintain her friendly relations with us." Later, Calhoun argued that Congress should focus on promoting American trade, not American military power, and that the "very magnitude" of the appropriation "decides the question of the expenditure." He next claimed that this type of "internal improvement" pulled individuals away from "useful labor" and put them to work "in the unproductive service of the Government." According to Calhoun, this type of "executive patronage" was "the cause of the great and fearful change which is so extensively affecting the character of our people and institutions" by doubling "the number of those who live, or expect to live, by the Government." As engineers waited to resume work in Charleston Harbor, Calhoun erroneously stated that although it was it was true that "there are fortifications at Charleston…they are not for our benefit, for their loop holes are turned towards the city." Besides, the unfinished Fort Sumter was a "nuisance" that obstructed Charleston Harbor and caused erosion on Sullivan's Island.

While there is no question that many South Carolinians wanted the Federal government evicted from Charleston Harbor, there is no reason to take seriously Calhoun's assertion that his opposition to the fort related to "extravagant expenditures" or ideological misgivings over the nineteenth-century version of the welfare state. Indeed, as the one-time proponent of a strong Union, Calhoun advocated for the fortifications program and approved the construction of Sumter as secretary of war. Besides, Calhoun was one of those people who spent the majority of his professional career in the "unproductive service" of the government. In reality, his newfound objections were both political and personal. By challenging the construction of Fort Sumter, Calhoun could prove his commitment to South Carolina's radical politics, which in turn helped maintain his status as the most powerful man in the state. But with Calhoun, politics was always personal. In private correspondence, he admitted that his objection to the fortification system was part of a broader effort to weaken an old enemy, President Jackson. It is little wonder that Old Hickory said on his death bed that he had only two regrets in life: "I didn't shoot Henry Clay, and I didn't hang John C. Calhoun."[24]

2
ELEVENTH HOUR

Despite Calhoun's efforts, in 1840, Congress appropriated $25,000 for the construction of Fort Sumter. On November 22, 1841, all issues regarding ownership of the fort were settled when the Federal government was granted the title to 125 acres of harbor "land" recorded in the office of the Secretary of State of South Carolina. Soon, Captain A.H. Bowman with the Corps of Engineers assumed responsibility for the project and set up his headquarters at Fort Johnson. Immediately, Bowman began to revise the original design and discarded the plan to build the fort on a grillage of square timber, opting to build it on a solid granite foundation instead.[25]

In January 1841, the engineers got their money from Congress and work picked up in Charleston Harbor, the "first and most necessary step" being "the construction of a permanent wharf to facilitate the discharge of materials &c." While the wharf was being built, workers began leveling the sandbar to unload granite secured from New York and the Penobscot River in Maine. Bowman reported to the board of engineers that the "enrockment around the foundation has been pushed on as rapidly as the amount of stones received would permit."

During the summer, when the amount of granite received was insufficient to give employment to the lighters, Bowman had the boats used to haul shell and sand for filling the parade ground. The engineers were pleased that the Charleston area "furnishes an abundance of these materials at a cheap rate" and that "Bricks of an excellent quality may be made upon the streams flowing into this harbour."[26]

To produce the estimated seven million bricks to build Fort Sumter, Brewerton relied on a large pool of Cooper River producers, including Stoneys, Parkers, Graves & Prioleau and Hamlin. Though these handmade bricks tended to be a dull brown color, they were referred to as "Carolina Greys."[27]

The engineers continued to be dogged by a lack of raw materials. The granite stones that arrived were furnished under the contract used to secure granite for the Moultrie breakwater, which was "so drawn as to bind the Contractor to deliver all the granite which might be required for the public works in Charleston Harbour during the summer of 1841." The materials were insufficient, and an additional contract was entered into on September 21 with "Ins. P. Austin for the delivery of 5000 tons of Stone at $3 per gross ton.—Also a contract was entered into on the 18 of Sept with Mssr. Ellis & Mays of Boston for 7,000 tons of granite blocks at $4.75 per gross ton."

By 1851, over 109,000 tons of granite, as well as other rock, was delivered to the site for the foundation, esplanade and wharf.[28] Soon, Charlestonians could look east and see a fortress of granite and dull brick rising out of the Atlantic Ocean. It was spectacular. The fort occupied around 2.5 acres and was designed with a symmetrical ground plan employing five faces with truncated angles. The walls rose vertically on all five sides to a uniform height 55 feet above the harbor. The interior of the fort where troops assembled for drill and inspection, called the parade ground, covered about 1.25 acres. Four of the walls, varying in thickness from 5 to 12 feet, had two tiers of gun rooms in casemate, allowing engineers to pack large numbers of weapons into the fort, multiplying the structure's firepower and extending the range of its guns. The fifth side, the longest at just over 316 feet, included the officers' quarters and was armed only along the top parapet, a work of masonry forming a protective wall over which defenders fired their weapons. The barracks for the enlisted men paralleled the gun rooms on the flanks. The scarp-wall was five feet thick but was backed by the arches and supporting piers of the casemates. A sally port (the main gate for the post) on the gorge opened on a stone quay and a 171-foot-long pier. At the water's edge, on the other faces of the fort, the rock foundation rose gently and terminated at the base of the vertical brick scarp-wall with a ledge 10 feet wide.[29]

The weapons that would arm the fort were based on new designs that increased the size, power and reliability of previous pieces. The old smoothbore cannon had a maximum range of one mile if fired at a five-degree elevation and could be loaded with solid iron shot or explosive shells. These standard forty-two- and thirty-two-pounders were designed to breach the hulls of wooden warships by flat trajectory or ricochet fire, but they

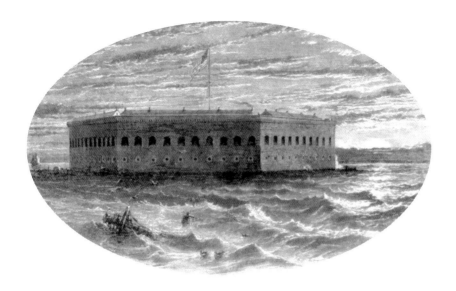

Fort Sumter occupied around two and a half acres and was designed with a symmetrical ground plan employing five faces with truncated angles.

could also fire shell, case shot, grape and canister. They were augmented by advanced cast-iron smoothbore pieces called columbiads. These guns were made in ten- and eight-inch calibers, which tripled the range of American armaments—the ten-inch model reached three miles.

Cannons were also notoriously unreliable and prone to burst when firing, oftentimes injuring or killing the operators. Artillery engineers also troubled themselves with aesthetics, adding moldings, rings, handles and other embellishments that did nothing to help the design and almost certainly made them more expensive to produce. By the 1850s, cannon founders tossed out the ornamentation and began experimenting with more reliable and powerful designs. U.S. Army Ordnance officer Thomas J. Rodman was at the vanguard of artillery engineering and began modifying American pieces just as Fort Sumter was taking shape. He determined that during the casting of large iron cannons, the sequence of cooling and hardening, which began at the outer surface and progressed toward the interior, left the finished gun with a pattern of stress directed toward the exterior. Since the pressures associated with firing were also directed radially outward from the bore, the total stress at the moment of firing sometimes exceeded the gun's limit of strain and caused the weapon to burst. He resolved this problem by circulating cold water through the hollow core of the casting, essentially

Artillery like this fifteen-inch Rodman columbiad was based on new designs that increased the size, power and reliability of previous pieces.

reversing the process. Rodman's design changes, along with advances in machinery, casting and higher-quality iron, played the leading role in reducing the instances of guns bursting and made it possible to produce bigger, more powerful guns. These design changes were materializing just as South Carolina began to talk of secession again.[30]

Fort Sumter and the Second Secession Crisis

Despite appearances, military commanders knew it would be years before Sumter was ready for self-defense. And self-defense, not protection of Charleston Harbor, was what they had on their minds in 1853.

On May 13, 1851, Lieutenant Colonel J. Erving with the Second Artillery sent a confidential letter from Fort Sumter to Fort Johnson asking for additional troops, including "two or three companies of artillery to Fort Sumter, for its protection."[31] The danger didn't come from America's foreign adversaries. Only four miles from the fort, from May 5 to May 8, 442 delegates from thirty-nine organizations assembled for the Southern Rights Association's meeting to discuss breaking with the Union. The rhetoric was incendiary with the association declaring, "We regard the position of the Southern States in this Confederacy as degraded and ruinous. The manifest tendency of those systematic aggressions which they have suffered for many years past is to subvert the institution of slavery…We see no remedy and no safety for the South in the present Union."[32]

Reconvening in July, the association resolved:

> *In view of the humiliating condition of the Slaveholding States in this Confederacy—their rights violated—their Institutions proscribed—their character vilified—their offers of compromise rejected—and in view of the still greater dangers which are impending over them, we believe the time has come when this Union should be dissolved, and a new Government organized on the basis of a Southern Confederacy.*

The document warned that if the Federal government moved to stop South Carolina's exit from the Union, "it would light up a blaze of civil war, which could never be extinguished."[33] This was no mere abstraction or empty threat. That year, the South Carolina legislature appropriated $350,000 to purchase weapons and munitions, a sum that doubled the state budget and increased state taxes by 50 percent.[34]

While Erving's request for soldiers and artillery was forwarded to General Totten, Kurtz prepared Fort Sumter for the arrival of additional troops. At that time, only a caretaker lived at Sumter, and it would be necessary to build quarters and barracks for the soldiers. The War Department was also informed that the gate of the fort entrance, located four feet within the outer plane of the scarp, was vulnerable to attackers. With South Carolinians threatening to exit the Union and likely

Robert Barnwell Rhett devised a scheme to seize the harbor forts under the pretext that their reinforcement by the Federal government was a threat to the city.

seize Federal fortifications in the process, the design required immediate alternation, or the Federal government risked losing Fort Sumter to local militia. This was complicated by the fact that Charleston had no stonemasons capable of doing, or perhaps willing to do, the work. Kurtz wrote his superiors that "to lay the traverse circles at Fort Sumter—I shall probably be obliged to get them [masons] from the North—incurring the expense of their passage out & back."[35]

As engineers worked to make the fort battle ready in the summer of 1851, South Carolina's radicals and cooperationists engaged in a vicious political fight to decide the fate of the Union. For over twenty years, the issue of secession divided the state, but for Fire Eaters such as Robert Barnwell Rhett, the time had come. Once the southern states left the Republic, they would create an empire that included Mexico, Cuba, Central America, the Caribbean and Brazil. This confederacy would challenge not only the United States but also the empires of Europe in landmass and economics. But there were problems. For one, most South Carolinians weren't sold on the idea of disunion, especially if the rest of the South wasn't onboard. Furthermore, a slave-based empire that stretched as far as South America struck most as ridiculous.[36]

This picture shows the guns of Fort Moultrie with Fort Sumter seen in the distance.

In June 1851, Rhett believed he finally had the spark that would save his dream of a southern empire. Fearing that Federal installations in Charleston would be seized by South Carolina, President Fillmore informed the commander of Fort Moultrie and Castle Pinckney that these facilities were to be immediately reinforced. With rampant rumors and fears among the locals, the commander also decided to suspend the traditional celebration at the fort commemorating the Revolutionary Battle of Fort Moultrie (June 28). Rhett pounced on these alleged provocations and, in a series of speeches, chastised his fellow Charlestonians for cooperating with the Federal commander by moving the commemoration. Their ancestors, he said, answered threats to their liberty by fighting not by having a picnic. He told the audience, "Let them come on" and ended his remarks with a challenge to other slave states to join South Carolina in ridding themselves of their Union overlords. All July and August, he hammered away at the issue, certain that the South would take action. To Rhett's surprise, the voters responded to his proposals with a collective yawn.

With much of the South regarding him as a lunatic or, worse, a buffoon, what Rhett needed was action. It was at this time that he devised a scheme to

seize the harbor forts under the pretext that their reinforcement was a threat to the city. He reckoned that when the U.S. military was deployed to South Carolina to retake them, the remaining southern states would get off the fence and he'd have his revolution. When the proposal was put to Governor Means, he refused to sanction such an action, declaring that only after secession could South Carolina confiscate these facilities. Rhett's plan was dead on arrival, and all he could do was take to the pages of the *Charleston Mercury* to whine about the state's failure to capitalize on this opportunity in the hope that some spontaneous attack might occur on the forts.[37]

In April 1852, Rhett and the other radicals were shut out of the state convention. No amount of demagoguery or grandstanding could breathe life into their moribund campaign. In districts where slaves were concentrated, the votes came in heavily in favor of the radicals, but the upcountry and Charleston voted in favor of cooperation with the Federal government, leading Edmund Bellinger from Barnwell District to remark that the radicals should follow Napoleon's example in Moscow and burn the Holy City. For his part, Rhett, who resigned his Senate seat in the wake of the loss, complained that the cause of secession failed because of the stupidity and fecklessness of the "the more ignorant class." Putting aside Rhett's patrician class rhetoric, simply put, the rest of the state was tired of the issue of secession, and by 1853, South Carolina turned to other matters. For the first time in years, the issue of slavery disappeared from the state's political discourse.

It wasn't to last.[38]

The *Echo* Affair

On August 21, 1858, the USS *Dolphin*, captained by John Newland Maffit, was patrolling for illegal slave traders when it spotted the *Echo* moving up the northern coast of Cuba. After the *Echo* was hailed, it tried to outrun the warship but dropped anchor when the Federal ship threw a shot over her bow. The *Dolphin*'s crew discovered 300 slaves below deck, mostly men and boys chained in the spoon position and starving. They had been purchased by Captain Edward N. Townsend as the agent for the Almeida firm, a front for Spanish nationals who trafficked Africans to Brazil. After moving north up the Angolan coast, Townsend made the purchase of 455 Africans at Cabinda at the mouth of the Congo River, paying six yards of cloth for each individual. Conditions on the *Echo* were beyond inhumane, with 144 captives dying during the thirty-five-day crossing of the Middle Passage, their bodies tossed to the sharks that followed the slavers.[39]

Captain Townsend and his crew were arrested, chained and sent to Charleston in September 1858 to stand trial for piracy. A guilty verdict meant death. The Charleston press was apoplectic. The *Courier* reported:

> *The slave crew were carried to our District jail this day handcuffed. Think of that!—Twenty men carried handcuffed through the streets of a slave-holding city by the President of the Young Men's Christian Association! And for what? For purchasing negroes in Africa and bringing them to the New World. For rescuing undying souls from the night of the heathen barbarism and transporting them to the full blaze of the Christianity of the Nineteenth Century.*

An editorial from the *Columbia Guardian* joined the Charleston papers, writing, "The slaves on board the *Echo* were regularly sold by the Africans and purchased by the captain of the *Echo*. They were therefore his bona fide property, and we think the officers of the *Dolphin* committed piracy."[40]

The captain of the *Echo*, Edward N. Townsend, purchased 455 Africans at Cabinda at the mouth of the Congo River, paying six yards of cloth for each individual.

The Africans, described by one witness as manacled "walking skeletons," were initially quarantined at the city jail. The next day they were taken into the custody of U.S. marshal Daniel Heyward Hamilton and housed at Castle Pinckney before being moved to Fort Sumter beyond the reach of local authorities. John Maffitt, captain of the *Dolphin*, reported that upon reaching Fort Sumter, the Africans began falling down from "disease and decrepitude," and some were so weak they could not walk. According to Maffitt, "privation of every kind, coupled with disease, had reduced all of them [the Africans] to the merest skeletons, and to such a state of desuetude and debility that on entering the fort they could not so much as step over a small beam one foot high in the doorway, but were compelled to sit on it and balance themselves over."

Their removal to Sumter did nothing to quell the excitement surrounding the *Echo*, and the city was hot with rumors that the Africans were to be absorbed into the local slave population, by force if necessary. One resident wrote in his diary, "All sorts of plans, schemes and projects, legal and illegal are broached and discussed as to the best means of getting them on shore, for once they are on shore they are free from U.S. laws and must come under jurisdiction of the State. They would find their way to plantations rapidly then." Predictably, Rhett's *Mercury* said that to return the Africans to their home continent would be a "wanton insult" to slavery and added there were buyers willing to offer $50,000 for the lot. Besides, slavery in South Carolina was preferable to freedom in Africa. While the local papers advocated for enslaving the Africans, U.S. marshal Hamilton, a one-time slave trader, wrote, "No one who has witnessed the amount of misery and suffering entailed upon these creatures by the horrors of the African Slave Trade… could for one moment advocate a traffic that ensures such inhumanity." A recent advocate for reopening the trade, he admitted that "a practical, fair evidence of its effects has cured me forever." After hearing the rumors that the abductees were going to be grabbed and sent to local plantations, Hamilton wrote that "but for the disagreeable necessity of firing on our own citizens, I would like no better fun, than to accommodate these pugnacious and valorous gentlemen, who are planning on rescuing the Africans from my hands."[41]

Most Charlestonians treated the Africans as a curiosity, taking tours to Sumter where they were paraded out in their tattered rags. The paddle steamer *General Clinch* delivered blankets, bacon and rice along with clothes donated by the city's residents, including local slaves. Foregoing the western garments, the slaves wore their own clothes and kept to themselves, speaking in their own languages and huddling in groups on the parade ground. A letter dated September 6 from John Johnson on Sullivan's Island to William T. Haskell reported that the Africans were "happy naked and dirty, the clothes which tender hearted ladies make for them being torn up immediately into ribbons to adorn their heads etc…They say themselves they will rather jump over board than be carried back to Africa." Captain John Maffit, who rescued the Africans from the *Echo*, saw things differently, recalling, "They huddled together closer than cattle, and slept in as close contact as spoons when packed together…it is impossible for you to understand their sad and distressed condition." Over the next few weeks, yellow fever claimed another thirty-five of the West Africans while the authorities debated what to do. Hoping to get the issue out of the papers, President Buchanan handed responsibility for the Africans to the Society for the Colonization of Free People of Color, created in 1816 to repatriate ex-slaves to Liberia. After a few weeks as the sole inhabitants of Fort Sumter, the group was retrieved by the steam frigate USS *Niagara* and departed for the five-thousand-mile voyage to West Africa. Another fifty-seven would die on the return trip.[42]

When manacled, emaciated Africans were the talk of the nation, it seemed like an inopportune time to talk about the virtues of slavery. Leionidas Spratt, the Charleston lawyer who represented the crew of the *Echo*, thought otherwise. Though Governor James H. Adams lost his battle to reopen the trade in 1856, Spratt considered the trial a perfect opportunity to argue that the slave trade was essential to the material progress, political power and social advancement of the South and perhaps all of humanity. He declared, "As equality was lost to the South by the suppression of the slave trade, so, would it seem, that the slave trade, would of necessity restore it." He believed that if slaves were made affordable by the opening of the African market, then "there is not an abolitionist there, who would not have purchased a slave, at a price approaching the cost of importation, and so purchasing a slave, there is not an abolitionist there who would not have become as strong a propagandist of slavery as ever lived." Once enlightened to the virtues of human bondage by the affordability of Africans, Spratt assured his antagonists that they too could be an approximation, albeit poor ones, of a southern gentleman and added, "I venture to affirm that there are no men, at any point upon the surface of the earth so favored in their lot, so elevated in their natures, so just in their duties, and so ready for the trials of their lives, as are the six million masters in the Southern States."[43]

As Spratt argued to reopen the African slave trade, the crew of the *Echo* was brought to trial at the U.S. Circuit Court in Charleston, guaranteeing their exoneration. After a few hours of testimony, the judge instructed the jury to acquit, and a verdict of not guilty was delivered. A second attempt to indict was dismissed, settling the matter for good. Southern newspapers were unanimous in their approval of the verdict. The *Mississippian* said, "Under these enactments the *Echo* prisoners have been indicted, tried and fount not guilty. We rejoice at this result." Rhett's *Charleston Mercury* wrote that it would have been "inconsistent, cruel, and hypocritical in them to condemn men to death for bringing slaves into a community where they are bought and sold every day." Northern newspapers were also watching the trial, and few would have disagreed with the *Cleveland Plain Dealer*, which lamented, "At both ends of this Confederacy the Union splitters are at work. An American vessel, a slave trader, is caught in the very act of piracy upon the high seas. She is taken into a Southern port, her crew arrested, tried by a Southern jury and acquitted…thus the work of disunion goes on."[44]

3
HOUSE DIVIDED

In April 1860, the Democratic Party National Convention convened in Charleston, the most proslavery city in the country. Institute Hall was crowded with the men who would decide the fate of the Democratic Party and, ultimately, the nation. The radical disunionists, determined to divide the party ticket and hand the election to the Republicans, precipitated a walkout of eight southern states, declaring "Slavery is our King—Slavery is our Truth—Slavery is our Divine Right." The ploy was a complete success, and the convention ended on May 1 without nominating a candidate. The convention reconvened in Baltimore on June 18, and the Northern Democrats eventually selected Stephen Douglas as their candidate, while Southerners nominated John C. Breckinridge. In an election that included four candidates, Abraham Lincoln won the Electoral College with less than 40 percent of the popular vote.

When news of Lincoln's election reached Charleston, there was a call for immediate secession. No promise, concession or constitutional guarantee could arrest the momentum for outright and immediate disunion. The die cast, South Carolina began to prepare for war. On October 20, the Washington Light Infantry, an elite corps of Charleston militia led by Captain Charles H. Simonton, met to discuss the "threatening aspect of affairs" and promised its services to Governor William H. Gist. The offer was accepted, and on November 12, the governor dispatched troops to guard the U.S. Arsenal in Charleston in the event that the Federal garrison decided to arm itself.

In April 1860, the Democratic Party National Convention convened in Charleston, the most proslavery city in the country.

With South Carolina moving rapidly toward independence, President Buchanan could no longer ignore the growing crises and convened his cabinet to debate the situation. Secretary of State Lewis Cass and Jeremiah S. Black, the attorney general, were adamant that Charleston's forts should be immediately reinforced. Secretary of War John B. Floyd was equally determined to see the status quo maintained and through the assistant secretary of state let it be known "that with his opinions he never could and never would consent to the coercion of a sovereign State." Floyd thought there was no chance a mob would take the fort, but if it was the state that decided to take the Federal installations, he could see no recourse but to let them go.

When Floyd discovered Buchanan was determined to reinforce the forts in Charleston Harbor, he told the cabinet that "his mind was made up, that he would cut off his right hand before he would sign an order to send reinforcements to the Carolina forts, and that if the President insisted, he would resign." Jacob Thompson, secretary of the interior, agreed and said he would leave the administration if the president followed through. Assistant Secretary of State William Henry Trescott, a Charleston attorney who rose to his position under Buchanan during the six months prior to secession and was an important intermediary between South Carolinians and President Buchanan early in the Fort Sumter crisis, was sent to Charleston to reassure South Carolinians that normal reprovisioning would continue while a solution was found. If he found that these actions would precipitate a fight, he was instructed that not a "man or a gun" should be sent to the Charleston Harbor.[45]

On November 7, the secretary of war dispatched Major Fitz John Porter of the adjutant-general's department to inspect the fortifications and report on the situation in Charleston Harbor. Porter found that a quarter of the garrison was under arrest or in confinement for disciplinary reasons. The major also found that Fort Moultrie had no sentinel to guard against an attack and that the:

> *unguarded state of the fort invites attack, if such design exists, and much discretion and prudence are required on the part of the commander to restore the proper security without exciting a community prompt to misconstrue actions of authority. I think this can be effected by a proper commander, without checking in the slightest the progress of the engineer in completing the works of defense. All could have been easily arranged several weeks since, when the danger was foreseen by the present commander.*

It was decided that Colonel Gardiner would be replaced with Major Robert Anderson, a trim, graying Kentuckian and veteran of the Mexican-American War. It was reckoned by Buchanan that Anderson, who once owned slaves and was married to a girl from Georgia, was the best choice for the assignment given the circumstances.[46]

While Anderson was en route, Brevet Colonel John L. Gardiner, at the urging of his officers, decided to retrieve arms from the arsenal on November 8. Gardiner knew he was already under surveillance by state troops and decided to send his men in civilian clothing to collect musket cartridges, percussion caps, primers and hand grenades under the cover of darkness. When the soldiers arrived at the arsenal, a mob was waiting, and it forced the Federal troops to beat a hasty retreat from the city. The governor responded by sending a telegram to Washington saying that if the removal of the ammunition was by order of the War Department, an attack on Federal installations was imminent. Hoping to deescalate the situation, Secretary

When Robert Anderson reached Charleston Harbor on November 22, the South Carolinians were already preparing for war.

Floyd replied that "no such orders have been issued, and none such will be issued under any circumstances."

When Robert Anderson reached Charleston Harbor on November 22, the South Carolinians were already preparing for a fight. Railroad iron was used to build an ironclad water battery for use in the harbor and a land battery on Morris Island. An elaborate set of signals was established for communications between the fortified islands and the city. The system included the use of Secessionville lighthouse and Saint Michael's Church steeple in Charleston as observation points. The Federal garrison felt the noose tightening, and one officer recalled, "We believed that in the event of an outbreak from Charleston few of us would survive; but it did not greatly concern us, since that risk was merely a part of our business, and we intended to make the best fight we could."[47]

With South Carolina moving toward a convention to decide the question of secession, President Buchanan instructed Assistant Secretary Trescott to tell Governor Grist that he felt obligated to send reinforcements. In a letter to Grist, Trescott said that the president's personal honor was at stake and that he was going to send men and arms to the forts even if it lead to war. The governor replied on November 29, 1860: "I have found great difficulty in restraining the people of Charleston from seizing the forts, and have only been able to restrain them by the assurance that no additional troops would be sent to the forts, or any munitions of war." The governor warned that if President Buchanan sent in reinforcements, "the responsibility will rest on him of lighting the torch of discord, which will only be quenched in blood."[48]

At that moment, Fort Sumter could, at short notice, mount 70 percent of its armament, and the magazines contained forty thousand pounds of powder and a full supply of ammunition for one tier of guns. It was, in Anderson's estimation, time to garrison Fort Sumter. He wrote to the U.S. adjunct general on November 23, 1860: "This work is the key to the entrance of this harbor; its guns command this work, and could soon drive out its occupants. It should be garrisoned at once."[49]

Anderson also wanted Fort Moultrie—already a wreck, with cows grazing along its earthen ramparts—improved, and the sand cleared from the exterior walls of the fort. These requests were often ignored, but Secretary of War John B. Floyd, a Virginian and secessionist sympathizer, appropriated $150,000 for Moultrie and $80,000 for Sumter claiming there was danger of war with England over Mexico. This was, of course, nonsense. Captain Abner Doubleday, a New Yorker and a veteran of the Mexican-American and Seminole Wars, then the second-highest ranking officer after Major Anderson, correctly deduced that the secretary's sudden "zeal to put the harbor of Charleston in condition" was so it could be "turned over to the Confederate forces." His suspicions were spot on. The secretary was already shipping heavy guns and ordnance to arsenals throughout the South, not for the defense of Federal installations, but so they could be seized by the southerners in advance of hostilities.[50]

By November 30, John Gray Foster, a career military officer and one-time assistant professor of engineering at West Point, had 115 men working on the fort, and the arrival of flagging stone allowed work on the embrasures to commence. There was sufficient stone to cover breakage, which Foster estimated to be 2.5 percent. Fort Sumter was beginning to take on a finished look but was not prepared for war. The barracks were still unfinished, and only 15 of the 135 guns planned for the gunrooms and upper terreplein were mounted.

The work at Sumter did not go unnoticed in Charleston, and an adjutant of a South Carolina regiment applied to Captain Foster for the names of the workers employed at the fort. Foster refused to give them, stating they had no right to make such demands, as the men were in the pay of the Federal government. Anderson now felt that an attack on Moultrie was imminent and reported to Washington that there were "intelligent and efficient men in this community who, by intimate intercourse with our army affairs, had become perfectly acquainted with this fort, its weak points, and the best means of attack." When a detachment was sent to Charleston to secure a six months' supply of food, one officer recalled, "The secessionists could hardly be restrained from attacking us, but the leaders kept them back, knowing that our workmen were laboring in their interests, at the expense of the United States." It was at this time that Foster proposed to connect a powerful Daniels battery with the magazine at Fort Sumter by means of wires across the harbor floor from Fort Sumter to Fort Moultrie so they could blow up Sumter should the South Carolinians try to seize it.[51]

Major Anderson could no longer be left without instructions, and Major Don Carlos Buell of the adjutant general's department was summoned on December 7 to meet with Secretary of War Floyd to discuss how they would proceed. Afterward, Buell departed for South Carolina and verbally told Anderson:

> *You are carefully to avoid every act which would needlessly tend to provoke aggression; and for that reason you are not, without evident and imminent necessity, to take up any position which could be construed into the assumption of a hostile attitude. But you are to hold possession of the forts in this harbor, and if attacked you are to defend yourself to the last extremity. The smallness of your force will not permit you, perhaps, to occupy more than one of the three forts, but an attack on or an attempt to take possession of any one of them will be regarded as an act of hostility, and you may then put your command into either of them which you may deem most proper, to increase its power of resistance. You are also authorized to take similar steps whenever you have tangible evidence of a design to proceed to a hostile act.*[52]

On December 17, Captain Foster decided that the crews working at Castle Pinckney and Fort Sumter were at the mercy of a mob and headed to the arsenal to retrieve two guns for Sumter. He also sent word to the military storekeeper that he needed forty muskets to arm the workmen. Every movement of the garrison was being watched. The storekeeper reported to Foster that removal of the guns caused "intense excitement," and a military official of the state warned "violent demonstration" was inevitable should they not be returned. Unknown to Foster, Colonel Benjamin Huger made an earlier agreement with the governor that no arms would be removed and assured state authorities they would be returned. Captain Foster didn't know or care about whatever arrangement Huger had with state authorities and refused to send the weapons back. That decision would fall to his superiors, not the governor of South Carolina. That afternoon, Governor Francis Pickens tried to preempt any attempt by the Federal men to occupy Sumter and sent word to President Buchanan that he wanted to dispatch a garrison of twenty-five men to hold the fort.[53]

At four o'clock on the afternoon of December 18, 169 delegates met at Institute Hall in Charleston to debate secession. There was very little in terms of debate. It was a foregone conclusion that disunion was inevitable. Though most South Carolinians thought secession would be accepted peaceably, there were no guarantees, and just miles from Institute Hall, there were workmen in the pay of the United States putting the final touches on Fort Sumter. That day, Governor Pickens sent a letter to President Buchanan demanding the surrender of all forts, magazines and other Federal property in Charleston. Major Anderson felt the danger. As Pickens's demand was en route to Washington, he wrote to the rector of his church in Trenton, New Jersey:

> *This fort is a very weak one in its capacity of being defended; it is surrounded by houses that I cannot burn or destroy until I am certain that I am to be attacked, and I shall not be certain of it until the South Carolinians are in possession; but I have so little ammunition that I cannot waste it in destroying houses. And again, within 160 yards from the walls are piles of sand-hills, some of them higher than our fort, which will give the best and safest shelter for sharpshooters, who may pick off in a short time our band of sixty men—all we have.*

On December 19, a telegram was sent from Charleston to the assistant secretary of state and native South Carolinian William Henry Trescott, informing him:

> *Captain Foster yesterday removed forty muskets from the arsenal in Charleston to Fort Moultrie; great excitement prevails; telegraph to have the arms instantly returned, or a collision may occur at any moment. Three days will determine, in convention, peace or war, and this act, not instantly countermanded by telegraph, will be decisive. Not a moment's time should be lost. Telegraph immediately to me.*[54]

It was late at night when Assistant Secretary Trescott received the telegram, but time was of the essence. He traveled to the secretary of war's house and found Floyd in bed ill. The chief clerk of the department was instructed to telegraph Captain Foster to return the arms and confirm he had done so. The telegraph office was kept open all night awaiting his response. But by

By the time South Carolina passed the Ordnance of Secession, Anderson had determined to abandon Fort Moultrie, pictured here with Fort Sumter in the background.

then, it was a moot point. Anderson had already instructed Foster to return the weapons on the eighteenth, and the arms were back at the arsenal the next day. A telegraph from J. Johnston Pettigrew, aide de camp for the governor, was sent from Charleston to inform the assistant secretary of state that "the Governor says he is glad of your despatch, for otherwise there would have been imminent danger. Earnestly urge that there be no transfer of troops from Fort Moultrie to Fort Sumter, and inform the Secretary of War."

On December 20, President Buchanan named prominent attorney and Northern Democratic leader Edwin M. Stanton as his new attorney general to replace J.S. Black, who had been promoted to secretary of state to replace Lewis Cass. Stanton was a brilliant attorney, perhaps the most talented litigator in the country, and an unflinching unionist. He adamantly opposed southern secession and would be a powerful proponent of meeting the challenge militarily. As soon as the announcement was made, Buchanan received William H. Trescott, who had just resigned from the Buchanan administration and was back on behalf of Governor Pickens. Trescott delivered to the president the handwritten and sealed letter written by the governor on December 17. After reading the letter in the presence of the assistant secretary, Buchanan handed the letter to him to read. Trescott knew at once the danger. Pickens's demands were brazen even by his reliably supercilious and pig-headed standards. The subtext was clear: failure to surrender all Federal property would result in immediate military action. The assistant secretary knew Buchanan was insulted and would likely respond to the challenge with a strong military demonstration. Though the U.S. Army had few forces at hand, the navy was more than adequate to enter the harbor and siege Charleston. Trescott telegraphed the governor asking that he withdraw the letter, which Pickens did, no doubt with great reluctance.[55]

That evening, the ordnance of secession was unanimously approved and officially signed in a ceremony at the South Carolina Institute. The announcement was greeted with the ringing of church bells, salvos from cannon at The Citadel and a night of wild partying. Meanwhile in Washington, President Buchanan was enjoying an evening wedding reception when South Carolina congressman Laurence Keitt burst into the room and shouted, "Thank God! Oh, thank God!" It was now a settled matter. Whatever hope the president entertained that South Carolina might be brought back from the precipice was gone. Stunned, Buchanan slumped into a chair and asked that a carriage be called so he could convene his cabinet.[56]

Within hours of South Carolina's secession, all Federal facilities in Charleston Harbor were under siege. The only sensible decision for Federal officers was to move to Fort Sumter, which, if well provisioned and manned,

This political cartoon from the period shows what many in the North thought of South Carolina's "ultimatum" to the Federal government.

could command the harbor. This fact, according to Anderson, was not lost on state authorities: "Fort Sumter is a tempting prize, the value of which is well known to the Charlestonians, and once in their possession, with its ammunition and armament and walls uninjured, and garrisoned properly, it would set our navy at defiance, compel me to abandon this work, and give them perfect command of this harbor."[57] This fear was confirmed when Secretary of War Floyd ordered Anderson to mount the guns at Sumter, no doubt so they could be seized by South Carolina forces and turned on the Federal garrison at Moultrie.

By the time South Carolina passed the Ordnance of Secession, Anderson determined to abandon Fort Moultrie, and at sundown on December 26, 1860, he told his men to pack their things and prepare to move that night. After throwing together what they could in the twenty minutes allowed by Anderson, the Federal troops left Moultrie and rowed to Sumter, concealing their weapons under coats as they slipped by the patrol boats. Once they reached Sumter, Doubleday recalled:

We went up the steps of the wharf in the face of an excited band of secession workmen, some of whom were armed with pistols. One or two Union men among them cheered, but some of the others said angrily: "What are these soldiers doing here? what is the meaning of this?" Ordering my men to charge bayonets, we drove the workmen into the center of the fort. I took possession of the guard-room commanding the main entrance and placed sentinels.

As soon as all the schooners were unloaded, Captain Foster had all Southern sympathizers placed onboard and sent to the mainland. Meanwhile, troops secured embrasures, and the fort, as much as possible, was put into a defensible condition against any storming party. Once in position, a cannon was fired as a signal to the rear guard waiting at Fort Moultrie, who spiked the guns of the fort, burned the gun carriages on the front-facing Sumter and cut down the flagstaff.[58]

The next morning, a delegation sent by Governor Pickens appeared and demanded that Anderson return to Moultrie. Major Anderson was respectful, but there was no chance of his going back to an untenable position on Sullivan's Island. Sumter was the strongest and most strategic fortification in the harbor, but there was a lot of work to do if he planned

Once the transfer of troops to Fort Sumter was completed, a cannon was fired as a signal to the rear guard waiting at Fort Moultrie, who spiked the guns of the fort and burned the gun carriages on the front-facing Sumter.

to hold it. The fort's parade ground was, as one contemporary recounted, littered with "building materials, guns, carriages, shot, shell, derricks, timbers, blocks and tackle, and coils of rope in great confusion." Aside from a few guns in the lower tier, the fort's main guns were still not mounted. While they needed to be in place in the event of a bombardment, there were more pressing concerns. With the discharged workmen providing intelligence on troop numbers and the readiness of the fort, it was distinctly possible that the South Carolinians would storm Sumter using a raiding party. With that in mind, Anderson decided to brick up many of the lower embrasures. If the South Carolinians wanted Sumter, they'd have to use scaling ladders and come over the top.

Unprepared for Anderson's move, Pickens was embarrassed and retaliated by ordering the seizure of Castle Pinckney under the pretense that he was protecting "public property." On December 27, members of the Washington Light Infantry, the Meagher Guards and the Carolina Light Infantry under the command of Colonel James Johnston Pettigrew, commander of the First Regiment of South Carolina Rifles, boarded the steamer *Nina*, crossed the one-mile distance and docked at Castle Pinckney at four in the afternoon.

The South Carolina troops entered the fort using scaling ladders and found Lieutenant R.K. Meade in no mood for a fight. Colonel Pettigrew announced that by order of Governor Pickens, he was taking possession of the fort. Meade didn't recognize Pickens's right to seize the fort but lacked the men or arms to prevent it. Meade was paroled and left for Fort Sumter as the Palmetto flag from the *Nina* was raised over Castle Pinckney.[59]

Meanwhile, Major Anderson and Captain Doubleday stood on the parapet of Fort Sumter watching the seizure through their field glasses. Anderson was angry and sent word to Governor Pickens that he saw the seizure as an act of war, but he decided to stand pat and await orders. Meanwhile in Washington, Buchanan and his cabinet viewed Anderson's move as a disaster but refused to order the garrison back to an indefensible position at Moultrie. On the twenty-eighth and thirtieth, General Winfield Scott, head of the army, wrote to President Buchanan that Anderson needed reinforcements to hold Fort Sumter. When Secretary of War Floyd discovered that the president was considering the request, he resigned and headed back to Virginia, where he would later serve as a brigadier general in the Confederacy.

After South Carolina seized the Charleston Arsenal on December 30 and Fort Johnson three days later, Anderson finally took ownership of the

Castle Pinckney was the first installation seized by the Confederate military on December 17, 1860. This photograph was taken from inside the fort.

situation and ordered the fort's armament mounted. After several days, the garrison managed to get two ten-inch columbiads to the upper tiers using a pulley system, while a third was mounted as a mortar on the parade for the purpose of shelling Charleston. There were also four eight-inch columbiads that were mounted as mortars to shell Morris Island should the Confederates place batteries there. There were also several forty-two-, thirty-two- and twenty-four-pounders and some eight-inch seacoast howitzers, but there weren't enough men or ammunition to use them all. James Chester, a sergeant with Company E, First U.S. Artillery Regiment, reported that "moving such immense quantities of material, mounting guns, distributing shot, and bricking up embrasures kept us busy for many weeks. But order was coming out of chaos every day, and the soldiers began to feel they were a match for their adversaries."

They also had to keep the South Carolinians out of the fort, so the first order of business was mounting the main gate, which consisted of two heavy iron-studded gates guarded by an eight-inch seacoast howitzer loaded with double canister. They also mined the wharf with canisters of gunpowder that could be detonated inside the casemates. The esplanade, a broad promenade extending

A depiction of Fort Sumter on December 1860 from *Frank Leslie's Illustrated Newspaper.*

the length of the gorge wall on the outside and paved with blocks of granite, was also vulnerable and undefended. Flagging stone was stacked in the area and underlain with remotely detonated mines. Additionally, two eight-inch howitzers were mounted and aimed at the main entrance to sweep the esplanade.

The news soon spread across the city that Anderson was not only refusing to return to Moultrie but was also mounting guns and preparing to fight. "Major Anderson, U.S.A," concluded the *Courier*, "has achieved the unenviable distinction of opening civil war between American citizens by act of gross breach of faith." Using the platform of the *Charleston Mercury*, Robert Barnwell Rhett pressured Governor Pickens to attack Sumter without delay. When Pickens told him to pull together a group of soldiers and do it himself, Rhett declined on the grounds that he wasn't a military man, complaining,

Review of the volunteer troops in Fort Moultrie on Sullivan's Island in Charleston Harbor in the presence of Mrs. Pickens and Miss Pickens, the wife and daughter of the governor of South Carolina.

"No reasoning on earth can satisfy the people of the South that in these two months a whole State could not take a fort defended but by 70 men." Rhett kept up the heat to the point that Pickens asked, "Is there no way to control the *Mercury*?" Despite all the grumbling about the governor's irresolution, men and arms were pouring into the city, and one resident wrote in her diary that "the city seemed suddenly turned into a camp. Nothing was heard but preparations for war."[60]

By the end of December, southern cabinet members were leaving Washington, and the Northern press was roundly criticizing Buchanan for his inaction in Charleston. The situation growing desperate, Buchanan made plans to reinforce Fort Sumter by sending the warship *Brooklyn* to resupply the fort. It was later decided that the *Star of the West*, a shallow-draft steamer, would be sent instead with 250 volunteers and supplies. There is some confusion as to what happened next. A message was received from Major Anderson that he did not need to be resupplied. Scott seems to have countermanded the order that the *Brooklyn* should not be sent at all. Instead, he ordered that the *Brooklyn* should follow the *Star of the West* in the event the steamer was attacked. On January 7, the president received political cover when the House of Representatives passed a resolution supporting Major Anderson's move from Fort Moultrie to Fort Sumter. The following day, the last Southerner in Buchanan's cabinet, Secretary of the Interior Jacob Thompson, resigned but not before providing intelligence on the *Star of the West*'s mission to South Carolina.

The *Star* crossed the Charleston Bar at 1:30 a.m. on January 9 but could find no guiding marks. Proceeding slowly with lights off, Captain John McGowan spotted through the morning haze the lights of Fort Sumter at 4:00 a.m. and steered to the southwest for the main ship channel. At daybreak, he reported a steamer heading in their direction, "who, as soon as she saw us, burned one blue light and two red lights as signals, and shortly after steamed over the bar and into the ship channel." The soldiers were put below, and no one was allowed on deck except the crew. As they continued up the channel, the steamer heading toward them fired off warning flares. When the *Star* was about two miles from Fort Sumter, a battery on Morris Island flying a red Palmetto flag opened fire on the ship. According to the captain, the *Star* was flying the American flag at the time but, after the first shot, ran up a large American ensign at the fore. They continued on under the fire of the battery for over ten minutes, and Captain McGowan reported that "one shot just passed clear of the pilot-house, another passed between the smoke-stack and walking-beams of the engine, another struck the ship just abaft the fore-rigging and stove in the planking, while another came within an ace of carrying away the rudder." As the shells came, two steamers were dispatched from near Fort Moultrie, one towing a schooner, with the intention of intercepting the *Star* before it could reach the fort.

Fort Sumter's garrison was ordered to battle stations while Major Anderson and his officers held a conference in a laundry room on the terreplein of the sea flank. They were informed by Anderson that they had no orders from Washington and would be sitting this one out. Though the Union officers were unhappy with Anderson's decision, they could do nothing. After a few minutes of action, Captain McGowan realized he wasn't going to receive covering fire from Sumter and ordered the *Star of the West* to reverse course and return to New York.[61]

The mission was a fiasco for Buchanan, who for the remainder of his term was hammered from all sides. Congress would grant him neither the money for military supplies nor the authority to call up the military. After Congress adjourned, Buchanan could have used their absence to act but lamely claimed he could order no military action without the consent

Firing on the *Star of the West* by Confederate troops on Morris Island.

of the legislative branch. When Anderson informed his superiors that he needed twenty thousand men to take and hold Charleston Harbor, the War Department replied, "You will continue, as heretofore, to act strictly on the defensive, and to avoid, by all means compatible with the safety of your command, a collision with the hostile forces by which you are surrounded."[62] Even though a relief expedition stood ready in New York for weeks, the situation now seemed impossible to remedy. The government was paralyzed.

Events now moved with a speed hard to imagine. On January 14, Virginia's legislature called for a convention to decide on separating from the Union. Thinking the matter a formality, the legislature extended an invitation to the other states to attend the Washington Peace Conference to participate in a negotiated settlement on Fort Sumter. Three days before the conference convened on February 4, J.W. Hayne, a commissioner from South Carolina, presented the state's demand to President Buchanan to surrender Fort Sumter. On February 6, Hayne was informed by the secretary of war, Joseph Holt, that the administration would never handover Fort Sumter. If South Carolina wanted the fort, it would have to take it by force or wait to bring up the matter with Abraham Lincoln. Two days later, the provisional government of the Confederate States of America (CSA) was established in Montgomery, Alabama, with Jefferson Davis elected as president and Alexander Stephens as vice president.

Amid this tumult, on February 11, Lincoln set out from his Springfield home en route to Washington for his inauguration. In his brief but forlorn farewell address to his townsmen, Lincoln said, "My friends, No one, not in my situation, can appreciate my feeling of sadness at this parting…not knowing when or whether ever I may return." A tiring twelve-day train trip ensued, with stops scheduled for Indianapolis, Cincinnati, Columbus and Pittsburgh, plus a detour through Cleveland, Buffalo, Albany, New York, Trenton, Philadelphia and Harrisburg. Due to threats of assassination coming from every direction, security was tight, and Lincoln's movements were carefully guarded.

By the time Lincoln got underway, South Carolina governor Pickens informed the CSA secretary of state Robert Toombs that he was "prepared to take the fort [Sumter] or silence it." In addition to the floating battery, Pickens reported that he had "mortars and Columbiads at Fort Moultrie, and plenty of 32-pounders as well as mortars at Fort Johnson." He assured the secretary, "If the attack was commenced the fort should be taken at every hazard: and if resisted, the slaughter of the garrison was inevitable."[63]

On March 4, Lincoln delivered a firm, forceful inaugural address. Though he hoped to strike a conciliatory tone, stating the he had no wish to interfere with the question of slavery in the Southern states, he was explicit in his desire to see the Union preserved. In the interest of the nation's integrity, Lincoln resolved to "hold, occupy and possess the property and places belonging to the government." In Charleston, Lincoln's address was received as expected with one resident declaring the speech "stupid…and insolent, and is everywhere considered as a virtual declaration of war." Governor Pickens apparently shared the sentiment and telegraphed the Tredegar Iron Works in Richmond, Virginia, on Inauguration Day: "Please send 400 shells for Dahlgren guns in addition to those already ordered."

The day after assuming the presidency, Lincoln was debriefed on the situation in Charleston Harbor. A report from the War Department relayed the message from Major Anderson that he was surrounded by battle emplacements and needed substantial reinforcements to hold Sumter. He also needed to be resupplied within six weeks or the men would have to go on short rations. In the letter, written on the day of the inauguration, Anderson reported that he was no longer allowed to buy food in Charleston to supplement their supplies. Joseph Holt, Buchanan's secretary of war, told Lincoln that he knew of no way to meet Anderson's requests. General in Chief

The day after assuming the presidency, Lincoln was debriefed on the situation in Charleston Harbor.

Winfield Scott was brought in to read Anderson's communiqué and told the president, "I see no alternative but surrender, in some weeks."[64]

Lincoln did not realize that while he was soliciting advice and information on how to reinforce Fort Sumter, Secretary of State William Steward was reassuring Southerners, especially those in the border states, that Sumter would soon be surrendered. He was also meeting with representatives from Virginia and assuring them that the president would not reinforce or resupply Sumter. To make matters worse, Seward was assuming much of the actual military operations related to Sumter. He reasoned that if the fort was surrendered, then cooler heads would prevail in the border states and perhaps even the Confederate states could be brought back into the fold. In the meantime, Lincoln was polling his cabinet members about whether he should send supplies to Fort Sumter and discovered that most thought it should be surrendered. The situation was growing desperate. Anderson said that, at best, he could hold the fort until April 15. Meanwhile, Stephen Hurlbut, a native of Charleston, informed Lincoln that "the sentiment in both the city and the state for Union was dead, that a separate nation is a fixed fact."[65]

On March 1, 1861, Brigadier General P.G.T. Beauregard, native Louisianan and graduate of West Point Class of 1838, was ordered to Charleston by the Confederate War Department and directed to assume command of "all forces in and about Charleston Harbor" and receive into service "such forces tendered or volunteered not to exceed 5,000 men." Within days, he had inspected fortifications, issued orders and assumed command of the entire coast from Beaufort to Georgetown. Despite his larger responsibilities, Beauregard understood that his first order of business was getting his old instructor from West Point, Robert Anderson, out of Fort Sumter.[66]

Confederate authorities decided that on April 15, Sumter would be evacuated or seized, whatever circumstances determined. In the interim, South Carolinians wanted Anderson's assurance he would not cooperate with any attempted relief effort. As this was not at the captain's discretion, the request was denied. The two sides were now at loggerheads. Beauregard was given explicit orders by his president that, if Washington tried to resupply Sumter, "You will demand its evacuation and, if this is refused, proceed in such manner as you may determine to reduce it."

Mary Chestnut, whose husband, Colonel James Chestnut Jr., was second in command to General Beauregard, wrote in her diary that the town was "red hot with rumors." While she worried that "Any minute…cannon may open on us," she enjoyed dinners of pate de fois gras salad, biscuit glace and champagne with Confederate officers at the St. Cecilia Ball and at Louis Trezevant Wigfall's home. Daughter of a wealthy planter, Emma Holmes wrote that though she feared the "terrors of a civil war," she looked forward to attending the city's many parades and military balls. On April 1, she wrote in her diary: "We walked to visit the fortifications…the gentlemen had provided us with fruit cake and champagne for lunch. The dinner was laid in a tent and was very nice, but camp life was shown by the deficiency of china." The following day, she noted, "We went to dinner about two o'clock in a large tent in the garden." The dinner consisted of "boned turkey, ham, lobster, salad, etc, but it was also laid in camp fashion—all the dessert being on at the same time…fresh preserved peaches, jelly and pound cake and afterwards ice cream and of course champagne and wines."[67]

A correspondent with *New York Times* marveled at the lack of seriousness among the city's elite. "The more I see of the men of Charleston," he wrote, "the more convinced I am that very many of them act, talk, and behave like perfect children." Though the people of the city assailed him as a propagandist for "a vile Black Republican sheet," they still allowed him into their homes and went out of their way to give him "exclusive information, and socially open to him their hearts, their homes, and even their purses." He determined that South Carolina in general and Charleston in particular was a "sublime mystery" and could not be "measured by any of the common-sense rules that govern one in their intercourse with ordinary people." After the war, he suggested that "some acute physiologist" be sent to the city to "give us a proper analysis of them, so that when another crisis comes, we shall be better prepared to meet it."[68]

On March 21, Ward H. Lamon, a personal friend of Lincoln, was dispatched to Charleston to size up the situation. He was informed by one of the city's last unionists, James Petigrue, that public sentiment favored immediate disunion and that "peaceable secession or war was inevitable." Meeting with Governor Pickens, Lamon was informed that any attempt to resupply Fort Sumter meant war.

Upon Lamon's return to Washington on March 28, Lincoln realized time was running out for the garrison. It was just reported in the *New York Tribune* that the *Brooklyn* was headed to Fort Sumter with men and provisions. Of course, the public and, obviously, Scott feared this would precipitate an armed confrontation. The Confederates vowed to allow no provisions into the fort. When Scott learned of the threat, he sent a message to Lincoln: "Let Sumter go and Pickens too!" When the cabinet was assembled and informed of Scott's message, most members met the news in stunned silence.[69]

Another cabinet meeting convened on March 29. The discussion was now about confrontation, not compromise. After the meeting ended, Lincoln wrote on the bottom of Captain Fox's communiqué to Secretary of War Cameron that "an expedition, to move by sea be got ready...as early as the 6th of April next...and you should cooperate with the Secretary of the Navy for that object." The order was signed, and duplicates were sent to the appropriate parties. Fox soon headed to New York to prepare the expedition. On Monday the eighth, two days after the relief mission left Brooklyn Navy Yard, emissaries for President Lincoln arrived in Charleston and hand-delivered his message to Governor Pickens.[70]

Pickens telegraphed Lincoln's message to Montgomery, where President Davis convened his cabinet. Its recommendation was clear and nearly unanimous: Beauregard must issue Anderson an ultimatum to surrender; if Anderson declined, Beauregard must take the fort. Only Robert Toombs, the Confederacy's secretary of state, argued against the response, writing to President Jefferson Davis in a memo: "The firing on that fort will inaugurate a civil war greater than any the world has yet seen...You will lose us every friend in the North. You will wantonly strike a hornet's nest, which extends from mountains to ocean. Legions now quiet will swarm out and sting us to death. It is unnecessary. It puts us in the wrong. It is fatal."[71]

On April 10, three members of Beauregard's staff, led by Colonel Chestnut, informed Major Anderson to surrender or Confederate guns would fire on Fort Sumter. The major answered that he was willing to hand over the fort provided the garrison could leave under arms and fire a salute to the American flag before departing. Unwilling to take yes for an answer, the delegation rejected Anderson's terms and departed for James Island. On April 11, and again the next day, Anderson refused to surrender. He was informed by Chestnut at 3:30 on the morning of April 12 that he was to hand over the fort or firing would commence immediately. Anderson replied to Beauregard's emissaries: "Gentlemen, if we do not meet again in this world, I hope we may meet in the better one."

Working from a battery at Fort Johnson, the order was given. At 4:30 in the morning, the first shot arced into the air and burst about one hundred feet above Sumter. Mary Chestnut heard the boom roll over the harbor and "sprang out of bed, and on my knees—prostrate—I prayed as I never prayed before." Under light drizzle, the entire city headed to the water to watch the fight. One correspondent reported, "The guns were heard distinctly, the wind blowing in shore. Sometimes a shell would burst in mid air, directly over Fort Sumter. Nearly all night long all the streets were thronged with people full of excitement and enthusiasm. The house-tops, the Battery, the wharves, the shipping, in fact every available place was taken possession of by the multitude."[72]

In the harbor, the outlines of the fort could barely be distinguished as the drizzling rain obscured the view and caused the smoke of the heavy guns to drift in low, listless clouds. Inside the fort, it was apparent by midafternoon that the garrison was in for a tough fight. Sumter was being hammered from three sides, and the upper exposed section of the fort suffered from the 2,500 shells fired from the Confederate batteries that day. The bombardment tapered off at night. By daybreak, the rain cleared, and the "morning rose clear and brilliantly beautiful." The firing was brisk as soon as the fort could be seen, and by 8:00 in the morning, Sumter's officers' quarters were ignited by a series of direct hits. Three hours later, one-fifth of the fort was on fire, and the wind drove the smoke in dense masses into the area where the Federal soldiers were sheltered. James Chester recalled:

> *We were not sorry to see the quarters burn. They were a nuisance. Built for fire-proof buildings, they were not fire-proof. Neither would they burn up in a cheerful way. The principal cisterns were large iron tanks immediately under the roof. These had been riddled, and the quarters below had been deluged with water. Everything was wet and burned badly, yielding an amount of pungent piney smoke which almost suffocated the garrison.*

Soon the fire was threatening to overtake the magazine, and if it went up, the Federal garrison was finished. They first tried to cover Sumter's stores of shells and shell grenades with wet blankets before deciding to throw all loose powder into the harbor. The tide was low and the powder barrels landed on the riprap just below the embrasures. The Confederates saw the barrels resting on the rocks above the waterline and targeted the pile, causing a massive explosion that pitched a lowercase gun out of the embrasure. Private John Thompson of the First U.S. Artillery later recalled that he "found the "heat and smoke…awful. Our magazine was becoming enveloped in flames, and our own shells were constantly bursting around us." There were no more wet blankets to toss on the ordnance, so a trench was dug in front of the magazine and filled with water to check the advance of the flames.

It was in the midst of the fight that ex-Senator Louis Wigfall of Texas visited the fort, rowed out by slaves while shells screamed overhead. After the perplexed gunners hailed him, he gained entrance by waving a white handkerchief from his sword. After a flag of truce was hoisted by the Federals, the firing died down, and negotiations began around three o'clock in the afternoon. Speaking on behalf of the Confederacy, which he had no authority to do, Wigfall told Anderson, "You have defended your flag nobly, Sir. You have done all that it is possible to do, and General Beauregard wants to stop this fight. On what terms, Major Anderson, will you evacuate this fort?" He assured Anderson that he would be allowed to leave the fort under arms and salute his flag on his departure. Thinking the matter settled, Wigfall returned to Morris Island, the hero of the hour.

Presently, a Confederate delegation including Stephen D. Lee, former Charleston mayor Porcher Miles and Roger Pryor arrived at Fort Sumter to see if Anderson was ready to surrender. When Anderson responded he negotiated terms with Wigfall, the delegation was incredulous and said the Texan was in no position to speak for General Beauregard. According to one witness, Anderson raised his hand in a "sweeping sort of gesture in the direction of Fort Moultrie" and told the Confederates, "Very well, gentlemen, you can return to your batteries." Meanwhile, Beauregard sent another delegation composed of South Carolina ex-governor John Lawrence Manning, Major D.R. Jones and Colonel Charles Allston to Sumter to offer essentially the same terms that Wigfall presented. The battle was over.

A *New York Times* correspondent described the scene in Charleston after the raising of the flag of truce as "indescribable; the people were perfectly wild. Men on horseback rode through the streets proclaiming the news, amid the greatest enthusiasm." As news of the surrender spread, the batteries in the city let loose a victory salute, and church bells rang throughout the city. About seven o'clock in the evening, it was announced that the terms agreed upon between General Beauregard and Major Anderson were accepted in Montgomery.

The next morning, Charlestonians piled onto anything that would float and made their way to Fort Sumter to watch the surrender. As the people of Charleston drunkenly celebrated the Confederate victory, the Federal garrison saluted the American flag at noon with a fifty-gun salute—accidentally killing one soldier, a young Irish immigrant named Daniel Hough, and mortally wounding Private Edward Galloway. Privates George Fielding, James Hayes, John Irwin and George Pinchard were also wounded by the misfire and were soon on their way to Charleston for treatment. The remaining Union troops formed ranks behind Captain Doubleday and marched through Sumter's main gate toward a waiting transport. In Charleston, the party was already underway, with one correspondent reporting, "The bells have been chiming all day, gun[s] firing, ladies waving handkerchiefs, people cheering, and citizens making themselves generally demonstrative. It is regarded as the greatest day in the history of South Carolina."

As Anderson and his garrison departed, the "stars and bars" took its place beside the Palmetto flag. Once the Federal troops vacated Sumter, Governor Pickens declared, "We have defeated their twenty millions. We have humbled the flag of the United States before the Palmetto and Confederate, and so long as I have the honor to preside as chief magistrate, so help me God, there is no flag on earth shall ever lower from that fortress those flags, unless they be lowered and trailed in a sea of blood." The enthusiasm was infectious, and few would have disagreed with one Confederate soldier who wrote, "It is firmly believed that we will have Washington in less than a month."

That afternoon, President Lincoln called for seventy-five thousand volunteer troops to put down the rebellion.[73]

4

WAR

As soon as the Confederates took possession of the fort, Sumter was put under the command of Lieutenant Colonel R.S. Ripley. Ripley was an Ohioan stationed in the 1850s on Sullivan's Island. There he met a rich widow, Alicia Middleton, and, like many Buckeyes, made the sensible decision to remain in Charleston. The balding, heavily mustachioed lieutenant colonel was the nephew of James Wolf Ripley, commander of the Federal troops in Charleston Harbor during the Nullification Crisis. History, it seems, was following some strange inverse symmetry.

Despite accusations that the lieutenant colonel enjoyed "intoxicating liquor" while on duty, Ripley pushed hard to get Fort Sumter into working order. Casemates at the main salient were finished. Armed and unused embrasures in the upper casemates were filled with brick. Anticipating an assault by Union gunboats, Ripley created an earthen rampart to protect the seaward-facing walls and fortified the gorge wall with stone masonry to a height of around fifteen feet. Near the eastern side of the sally port, engineers mounted two casemate howitzers to defend the pier. Lieutenant Colonel J.A. Yates devised a mechanism that allowed the garrison to traverse the guns with cranks and cogwheels. The hot-shot furnaces were rebuilt, and the brick soldiers' quarters on the interior of the eastern and western casemates were reconstructed, but at a reduced height. The officers' quarters were also partially rebuilt.[74]

On July 4, Charlestonians heard the sound of artillery, which most assumed to be a salute to independence from England. The next morning, the *Mercury* reported that they were "informed by the officers in command of these posts that no salute whatever was fired by them on the occasion." The forts were simply practicing the men. Readers were assured that officers of Fort Sumter knew the real Independence Day and "on the 20ᵗʰ of December next they shall not wait for orders" to fire their guns in honor of the Confederacy.[75]

In the months before the Federal squadron appeared off the South Carolina coast, the locals often traveled by boat to pay homage to the city's defenders. One Confederate officer reported that it "became an indispensible custom for Charlestonians to see the dress-parade and hear the band play at Fort Sumter…a tribute due both to the war spirit of the time and to the merit of a fine command." Many of the city's elites attended "garden and dinner parties, weddings, military balls, and informal picnics and supper dances at Fort Moultrie, Sumter and Pemberton." Men had their portraits made in their newly tailored uniforms. The women enjoyed picnics and "grand parties," and there was a minor scandal when it was discovered several ladies snuck off to watch Beauregard's staff dance the can-can.

Despite the heady enthusiasm, Beauregard, knowing it was only a matter of time before an offensive was opened up on Charleston, went to work building the "circle of fire" that defended the city. On December 18, the South Carolina General Assembly passed Act No. 4614, requiring slaveholders to provide laborers to Confederate military authorities "as may be demanded" for work on the state's coastal defenses. Nevertheless, demand exceeded supply, and Beauregard leaned hard on his soldiers to finish the job. Uninterested in the drudgery of spadework normally left to slaves, many of the Confederate soldiers put on civilian clothes and headed out of town. The *Charleston Mercury* posted thirty-dollar rewards for all deserters delivered to Fort Sumter or the Charleston jail. A typical description read, "1. JAMES HATCHEL, of Company D. Deserted from Fort Sumter. Said Hatchel is 31 years of age, 5 feet 7 inches high, grey eyes, black hair, fair complexion; is a native of Marion District, S.C., and enlisted at Fort Sumter." As the war took its toll in later years, the number of desertions escalated. One soldier reported that about twenty men had gone over to the enemy, but he did not blame them, "for we are not treated right by our officers. We are compaired [*sic*] to niggers….and they are taking to bucking and gagging the men for hardly any offense at all." By 1863, the problem was chronic, resulting in the execution of a deserter by firing squad at the Washington Race Course as an example to soldiers thinking of slipping past the pickets and heading home.[76]

Despite the desertions, the work picked up with Major General J.C. Pemberton driving timber piles into the shallow inner harbor and anchoring a boom of heavy timber logs, weighted and fastened with iron, across the channel between Forts Moultrie and Sumter. The arrangement proved unworkable due to weather and tides and was replaced with a three-cable rope obstruction designed to snare wheels and propellers of Union ships if they fought their way into the harbor. As a last line of defense, torpedoes, similar to mines, were placed in the harbor, and guns were positioned along the city's waterfront. As these improvements were pressed to completion, a telegraph cable between Forts Sumter and Moultrie was laid along the harbor floor. When it was completed, the two forts simultaneously fired a salute in honor of the event, the order having been transmitted from Fort Sumter over the wire to Fort Moultrie.[77]

Ironclads

Seven months after the Confederates opened their guns on Fort Sumter, Union troops returned to South Carolina. Leading a fleet of seventeen ships, Flag Officer Samuel Francis Du Pont entered the two-mile harbor mouth of the Broad River and drove straight for Port Royal. Defended by Forts Walker and Beauregard and supported by troops commanded by Brigadier General Thomas Francis Drayton on Hilton Head, the Confederate forts were engaged on November 7 with two hundred guns from the Union warships. After four hours of battle and sixty-one Confederate casualties, the forts were abandoned and Brigadier General Thomas W. Sherman's twelve thousand troops occupied the area.

Working from their beachhead at Port Royal, Union troops pushed north to take the "cradle of the Confederacy": Charleston. With the Confederates pulling back, the Northern troops met little resistance and one solider reported that all he saw was "stink weed, sand, rattlesnakes, and alligators. To tell the honest truth, our boys out on picket look sharper for snakes than they do for rebels." After a tough slog through the Lowcountry swamps, the Union troops were at Charleston's backdoor by June, and there were no more complaints about boredom. Though General Henry W. Benham's forces were turned back in a sharp fight at the Battle of Secessionville, it was a foregone conclusion that Charleston was fated for destruction, and one city resident remarked that it was not uncommon to hear "people gravely talk of setting fire to the city if they can not defend it."[78]

With General George McClellan bogged down in Virginia and General Lee checking the Federal offensive on the Yorktown Peninsula, President Lincoln set his sights on Charleston. On May 12, 1862, Secretary of the Navy Gideon Welles informed Du Pont: "This Department has determined to capture Charleston as soon as Richmond falls." Having succeeded in taking Port Royal with ease, the U.S. Navy Department decided to use the same strategy of seizing Charleston by a strong force of armored vessels with a coordinated attack on Folly and Morris Islands by Major General David Hunter's 11,500 infantry and six hundred artillery pieces.[79]

Under the command of Du Pont, the squadron rendezvoused at Port Royal and began planning the logistics for the attack. The Navy Department was sublimely confident of success, and on January 6, 1863, Secretary Welles informed Du Pont that "the *New Ironsides*, *Passaic*, *Montauk*, *Patapsco*, and *Weehawken* [iron-clads] have been ordered to, and are now on the way to join, your command, to enable you to enter the harbor of Charleston and demand the surrender of all its defenses, or suffer the consequences of a refusal." Though land-based forces would be deployed to the theater, Welles informed the admiral that "the Capture of this most important port, however, rests solely upon the success of the naval forces, and it is committed to your hands to execute." Though Welles understood that the city was of minimal strategic value, ideologically it was the heart of the Confederacy. Assistant Secretary of the Navy Gustavus V. Fox expressed that sentiment on June 3, 1861, writing to Du Pont that "the fall of Charleston is the Fall of Satan's Kingdom." Though Washington was eager to see the fall of Sumter avenged, Du Pont and his staff were skeptical of "this fighting by machinery," and he noted that in previous engagements, the monitors performed poorly against forts. The Navy Department entertained no such doubts, and Welles informed Du Pont that as soon as the city was taken, he was to dispatch a portion of the ironclads to attack Savannah "under the panic which will be produced by the fall of Charleston."[80]

In addition to the practical difficulties of his command, Du Pont needed to be mindful of enemies back in Washington. Chief among them was John Dahlgren, commander of the Washington Navy Yard. Under his direction, the navy established its own foundry to manufacture new weapons, and Dahlgren invented the Dahlgren gun, a powerful class of smoothbore cannon that became the standard weapon on Union naval vessels after 1856.

Though thin and delicate in appearance, Dahlgren possessed the trait the president admired most—guts. They instantly hit it off.

After befriending Lincoln, Dahlgren lobbied the president for Du Pont's job as commander of the South Atlantic Blockading Squadron and even had his allies in Washington ask Du Pont to allow him to lead the attack on Charleston. Du Pont was insulted, writing to Secretary Welles that "Dahlgren is a diseased man on the subject of preferment & position… he chose one line in the walk of his profession while…I chose another; he was licking cream as we were eating dirt & living on the pay of our rank. Now he wants all the honors belonging to the other but without having encountered its joltings—." Both Secretary Welles and his deputy, Gustavus V. Fox, were annoyed by Dahlgren's boundless ambition, though they saw him as possessing considerable talent. In his diary Gideon Welles wrote, "Dahlgren has asked to be assigned to the special duty of capturing Charleston, but Du Pont has had that object in view for more than a year and made it his study. I cannot, though I appreciate Dahlgren, supersede the Admiral in this work." Welles informed Dahlgren that Du Pont deserved the "honor of leading and directing these forces" and if he wanted to take part in the campaign against Charleston, he could command an ironclad. This was not the assignment Dahlgren had in mind, and he passed on the offer.[81]

As the weeks became months, Lincoln grew frustrated with the delays, and Du Pont was summoned to Washington in October 1862. President Lincoln first complained about the performance of U.S. troops at the Battle of Secessionville and then shifted the conversation to the Army of the Potomac. He was frustrated that Major General George McClellan was constantly asking for more troops, saying, "If you promise him those, he will call for ten thousand more." The implication was clear: the president would no longer tolerate timid officers. It was time to fight.

In February 1863, Lincoln dispatched Assistant Secretary Fox to South Carolina to get things moving. Though Du Pont doubted Charleston could be taken without a concurrent land attack by the army, Fox believed a single ironclad could reduce Sumter and force the city to surrender. After watching the monitors in action, Du Pont dismissed Fox's opinions as naïve and sent an officer to Washington to secure another three ironclads and more deck plating in advance of the attack. When Lincoln learned of the request, he sent a message to Du Pont, stating, "I fear neither you nor your officers appreciate the supreme importance to us of time. The more you prepare the more the enemy will be prepared."

Though "prepared for a repulse at Charleston," Lincoln could not tolerate Du Pont's foot dragging and told Secretary Welles that the admiral's tentativeness and "his constant call for more ships, more ironclads, was like General George McClellan calling for more regiments." As Du Pont dithered, the president's mood grew darker. In his diary, Secretary Welles wrote, "The President, who has often a sort of intuitive sagacity, has spoken discouragingly of operations at Charleston during the whole season. Du Pont's dispatches and movements have not inspired him with faith. Fox who has more naval knowledge and experience and who is better informed of Charleston and its approaches, which he has visited, and the capabilities and efficiency of our officers and ships, entertains not a doubt of success." Despite Fox's optimism, in the days before the attack, the president was in near despair at the thought of the attack on Fort Sumter. During a trip to see the Army of the Potomac, journalist William O. Stoddard reported that the president "seemed absorbed in the saddest reflections for a time; then, becking a companion to him, said, 'What will you wager that half our iron-clads are at the bottom of Charleston Harbor?' This being the first intimation which the other had had of Dupont's attack, which was then begun, hesitated to reply, when the President added, 'The people will expect big things when they hear of this; but it is to late—*too late!*'"

For Du Pont, there was no turning back. As he prepared the gunboats for the attack, he wrote to his wife that "the eyes of the nation and the government upon me and expectant, when the national heart is sore and impatient for a victory." Welles sent the admiral his three monitors in early March and a pointed letter directing Du Pont to get on with the attack. After lingering a few days in the North Edisto River for final preparations, he gave the order to pull anchor and the Federal squadron headed north.[82]

The squadron was seen from the walls of Fort Sumter on Sunday, April 5, and consisted of nine armored vessels. The monitors were armed with two guns, typically a fifteen-inch smoothbore and heavy rifle. Though it took about seven minutes to reload the weapons, the Federal crews believed this handicap was remedied by their fire power. The most formidable vessel was Du Pont's flagship, the *New Ironsides*, a steam frigate armed with twenty eleven-inch guns and a two-hundred-pound pivot rifle on its front deck. Colonel Alvin C. Voris with the Sixty-seventh Ohio Infantry said that the ship "could discharge a broadside of ten guns at short range every three minutes." The garrison at Fort Sumter acknowledged the arrival of the gunboats by raising its flags and firing a salute to Du Pont.

Though the admiral's plan was to advance that day, the weather didn't cooperate, forcing the fleet to remain at anchor about four miles southeast of Fort Sumter.

Sunrise on April 7 revealed a sparkling sea and cloudless blue sky: a perfect day for a fight. While Du Pont said he wanted to wait for the ebb tide at 10:20 a.m., the ship pilots cautioned to wait for the outgoing tide at 12:15 p.m. to aid in steering and prevent disabled vessels from drifting into the harbor. Immediately things started going sideways when the lead vessel, the *Weehawken*, weighed anchor, and an attached raft meant to protect against torpedoes became entangled with the grapnels attached to the bow. Requests to move ahead without the lead vessel were denied, and the gunboats waited until 1:45, by then working against the tide.[83]

London News correspondent Frank Vizetelly was present when a telegram from Colonel Rhett alerted General Ripley that the Union squadron crossed the bar and were moving up the channel. Ripley turned to Vizetelly and said, "Thank God, we shall soon know the issue of this fight." Through his field glasses, Vizetelly could see the turrets of the ships moving as they advanced up the channel and wrote that he "could almost hear the thumping of my heart against my ribs."

As the Union squadron struggled to gain steam, the garrison at Fort Sumter sat down to an early dinner. At Battery Wagner, the Confederates watched the squadron close on Fort Sumter, though neither the ironclads nor Wagner initiated the engagement. In the city, it was standing room only as men, women and children crowded the battery, wharves, windows and rooftops to watch the fight. Vizetelly reported that Charleston was eager to see the clash: "The non-fighting population of Charleston fall into their places, young girls with their negro nurse—a piebald medley of black and white…ladies in almost gala costume, are hastening to the battery promenade, from whence an unobstructed view of the harbor and forts."[84]

By 2:30 p.m., the garrison at Fort Sumter, in full dress-parade uniforms, moved to its guns. The garrison flag was raised from the northern salient. The white crescent and palmetto flag of South Carolina flew at the western angle of the gorge ramparts. The hoisting of the flags was followed by a thirteen-gun salute and the playing of "Dixie" by Sumter's regiment band. The fort's casemates were commanded by Major Blanding, while Lieutenant Colonel Yates, who had just arrived that morning, was charged with the responsibility of the open-air batteries and took up a position near the parapet of the southeastern angle to watch the movements of the Federal gunboats. All the while, the artillerists were waiting for the squadron to come into range of their guns, which were already fixed on a buoy placed at the turn of the channel about 1,120 yards from the fort.

The *Weehawken* came abreast of Fort Moultrie at 2:50 p.m., and the garrison could see a massive explosion of water alongside the *Passaic*. A moment later, the men heard the roar of a columbiad from Moultrie roll across the harbor. Moultrie's first shot sailed high, so the firing stopped as the artillerists adjusted the range. One correspondent watching from Sumter reported that the *Passaic*, second in line, swung its turret around and "an iron shutter glides aside, disclosing a dark port, which, in a few seconds, vomits forth a cloud succeeded by a crash that shakes the very ground we stand on." The *Weehawken* soon joined the *Passaic*, both fixing their fire on the eastern face of Sumter.

The first shot at Fort Sumter passed just over the heads of the Confederates firing the barbette guns on the right flank. The regimental flag on the gorge wall was hit, piercing it near the crossing of the two cannons in the center of its field.[85] The first shot to strike the fort landed at the eastern angle, sending bricks down on the heads of the Confederates. The shell struck with such force that its concussion could be felt on the other side of the fort. Another round landed near the base of the eastern wall and sent over the parapet a cascade of water that soaked the guns and garrison serving that area. Another shot breached the scarp-wall's upper-tier embrasures, setting ablaze the temporary soldiers' quarters on the eastern side of the fort. The fire was unexpected and threatened to overtake the overhead guns and the adjacent magazines. The fort's fire department, directed by Lieutenant Charles Inglesby, attacked the blaze, which was soon under control. Just as that crisis was resolved, a shell crashed into the western barracks setting it on fire.

At 3:00 p.m., the lead vessel reached the buoy, and the guns of Fort Sumter opened on the gunboats. Soon all the Confederate positions joined in. As the metal flew, the *New Ironsides*, believing that it was about to be grounded on the eastern edge of the ship channel, cut speed about a mile distant from Fort Sumter. While the ship floundered, the Confederates tried to detonate a torpedo boiler that was beneath the flagship, but it failed to explode. Behind it, the *Weehawken* and *Passaic* were confused and waited for the *New Ironsides* to resume speed and open fire on Fort Sumter. Instead, the vessel stalled and drifted to a distance of about two thousand yards from the fort. The *Catskill* and the *Nantucket* didn't slow sufficiently to account for the ship's loss of steam and were soon afoul of it. Now in total disarray, at 3:20 p.m. it signaled the remainder of the squadron to disregard its movements and move ahead.[86]

In the monitors, it was obvious within twenty minutes of action that, though well protected, their smaller guns lacked the offensive power to batter Fort Sumter into submission. Worse still, the ships' captains could see almost nothing from the small portholes and communication between the monitors was almost nonexistent as the view was obscured by smoke and the explosion of water as shells landed all around them. The Confederate artillerists soon had the range, and the *Weehawken* and *Patapsco* were struck by Confederate shells about once per minute, while they were able to get off only eighteen shots between the two in twenty minutes of action. For their part, the Confederate forts and batteries engaged more than one hundred of the heaviest guns they had at hand, "shooting their balls, their shells, and fiery bolts with deafening sound and shocks of powerful impact that surpassed all previous experience of war."

Commanding the *Passaic* was Percival Drayton, scion of the South Carolina Draytons who did the unthinkable and threw in with the Union. When his gunboat came opposite the center of Fort Sumter, he saw what he thought were obstructions crowding the channel and slowed his ship. Just as he was firing his fourth shot with the eleven-inch gun, the *Passaic*'s was struck twice in quick secession. Drayton reported that the gun was knocked out of action, rendering it, "wholly useless for the remainder of the action." The turret was subsequently jammed, and a heavy rifle shot hammered the upper edge of the turret "broke all of its eleven plates, and then glancing upward took the pilot house." With its guns knocked out of action and its turret and pilothouse wrecked, Drayton withdrew from action.[87]

As the *Passaic* fell back, the *Weehawken* continued to mix it up with Fort Sumter but didn't fare much better. It had its side-armor broken, exposing the wood beneath the iron plating, and soon its turret was also jammed and its eleven-inch gun knocked out of action. Behind it, the *Patapsco* stalled out and was wrecked by Sumter's guns. On its fifth shot, the rifled gun was disabled, the upper part of its armor loosened and its turret jammed.

With the flagship still in disarray, the four vessels of the second division moved to the front, led by the *Catskill*. Behind it, the *Nantucket* commenced firing on Fort Sumter at 3:50 p.m. but refused to move closer, fearing torpedoes. The *Nantucket*'s first fifteen-inch shot was fired from its revolving turret and was followed up with an 11-inch shell. One officer aboard the gunboat reported that they were soon "amid a perfect shower of 10-inch shot and shell, striking the *Nantucket* at every available point." After getting off only three shots, the *Nantucket*'s 11-inch gun was disabled, while the *Catskill*'s deck was severely damaged. For its part, the *Montauk* was slammed with fourteen shots on its side armor and another that damaged the pilothouse.

The *Nahant* and the *Keokuk* were last to join the fight, but their decision to engage Fort Sumter at close range meant they were in for a nasty beating. Captain John Downes Jr. took the *Nahant* into "the hottest fire of the forts" and managed to get off fifteen shots before the commander reported that the ship "began to suffer from the effects of the terrible and I believe almost unprecedented fire to which we were exposed."[88] After the gunboat was struck eight or ten times, the captain gave the signal to move in closer and promised the crew that "he would go in and fight hand to hand." As the *Nahant* moved up the channel, the Confederate shells smashed its turret and pilothouse and raked the ship's deck. Ship surgeon Charles E. Stedman reported that the "balls & shells & bolts rattled like hail upon us, every little while showers of water would fall upon us and down the turret." When artillery fire struck the pilothouse, bolts ricocheted around the interior of the ship, stunning the pilot. Edward Cobb, the helmsman and thirty-year veteran of the U.S. Navy, was injured with a fractured skull and died later that night. The shelling also disabled the ship's steering, and the *Nahant* ran the risk of being pushed by the tide onto a sandbar. After a flurry of activity within the gunboat, the crew got the steering fixed, and it limped away from the fight with the Confederates still firing as the vessel moved east.[89]

Distrusted by the rear admiral, the *New Ironsides* remained around 1,500 to 2,000 yards distant from Fort Sumter. About an hour into the fight, it started moving up the channel as if to join the battle. Once the gunboat was in range of Forts Moultrie and Sumter, the ship abruptly turned around and returned to a safe distance after throwing a few shots at Moultrie and Wagner. Though General Beauregard believed the Confederate guns put the *New Ironsides* out of action, an assessment after the battle revealed the Confederate fire had no effect, and the ship was not damaged either in its iron or its woodwork. The durability was confirmed when, five months later, it engaged Fort Moultrie at 1,200 yards and was undamaged despite being hit seventy times.

As the *New Ironsides* withdrew from the fight, Commander A.C. Rhind, commanding the *Keokuk*, considered the weakest of the gunboats, decided to move within 550 yards "bow on" from Fort Sumter and if "she proved invulnerable," one of its officers recalled, "we were prepared to fight the rebels at the mouths of their cannon." The captain's bravado was short lived. "The men were perfectly awe-stricken," reported the paymaster of the vessel, "Such was the roll of fire along the sides, that we could scarcely open the ports of the vessel to fire." In thirty minutes, the ship fired only three shots from the forward turret but was stuck ninety times. The turrets "were entirely penetrated by rifle-bolts and 10-inch round shot," while nineteen shots punctured just below the water line. Despite its condition, the crew managed to keep the engines running, allowing the *Keokuk*, fatally crippled, to move away from the Confederate guns. Though it managed to stay afloat throughout the night, the next morning, the ship sank at anchor off the southern end of Morris Island as the Rebels on the island tossed their hats and cheered. The Federals failed to scuttle the ship, and the Confederates later slipped in under cover of darkness and used a derrick and lifting tackle to pluck the massive Dahlgren guns from the *Keokuk*. The guns were later placed in their defensive batteries in Charleston Harbor.[90]

With the squadron in no condition to continue the fight, Du Pont issued the order to withdraw sometime between 4:30 and 5:00 p.m. The Union squadron kept up the fire initially, but as it moved east, its guns fell silent. For their part, the Confederate artillerists continued pounding away until the ships were out of range. On Morris Island, Battery Wagner, which didn't engaged as the squadron made its initial approach, opened up as the procession filed past.

As the Confederates spent the night strengthening Fort Sumter's firepower in anticipation of another attack, Du Pont conferred with his officers to assess the damage to his squadron. That evening, he decided to call off the attack and wrote the next morning to his U.S. Army counterpart, Major General Hunter: "I have attempted to take the bull by the horns, but he was too much for us. These monitors are miserable failures where forts are concerned; the longest was one hour, the other forty-five minutes, under fire, and five of the eight were wholly or partially disabled."[91]

Unaware that Du Pont was steaming south, President Lincoln sent new orders to Du Pont on April 13:

> *Hold your position inside the bar near Charleston; or, if you shall have left it, return to it, and hold it until further orders. Do not allow the enemy to erect new batteries or defenses on Morris Island. If he has begun it, drive him out. I do not herein order you to renew the general attack. That is to depend on your own discretion or a further order.*[92]

The following day, the president, believing another attempt was being planned against Charleston, sent a follow up message to Admiral Du Pont and General Hunter:

We wish the attempt to be a real one, though not a desperate one, if it affords any considerable chance of success. But if prosecuted as a demonstration only, this must not become public, or the whole effect will be lost. Once again before Charleston, do not leave until further orders from here. Of course this is not intended to force you to leave unduly exposed Hilton Head or other near points in your charge.[93]

The use of the word "demonstration" was surely not lost on Du Pont. At this point, it didn't matter. The admiral was already in Port Royal repairing the fleet. The fight was over.

Though the loss of life and property were negligible, the battle was a public relations fiasco for the Lincoln administration. When the media asked about the battle, the president, "with a downcast, haggard, bewildered look," told the reporters that he was "not pleased with the results." He was even more candid with another visitor, stating that "six months' preparation for Charleston was a very long grace for the thin plate of soup served in the two hours of fighting." For his part, Secretary Welles was furious with Du Pont. In his diary, Welles wrote, "We learn that after all our outlay and great preparations, giving him about all our force and a large portion of the best officers, he intends making no farther effort, but will abandon the plan and all attempts to take it. A fight of thirty minutes and the loss of one man, which he witnessed, satisfied the Admiral."[94]

Du Pont was finished. After a series of damning reports were leaked to the press by the secretary of the navy, Du Pont was cashiered on June 3 along with Major General David Hunter. On June 4, Major General Quincy Adams Gillmore, then recruiting volunteers in New York, was ordered to the Department of the South and tasked with taking Charleston. A talented member of the Corps of Engineers, he is described by a newspaper correspondent, as "a quick-speaking, quick-moving, soldierly man…a fine, wholesome looking, solid six footer, with big head, broad, good humored face, and a high forehead faintly elongated by a suspicion of baldness, curly brown hair and beard, and a frank open face." More importantly for President Lincoln, he liked to fight.

By June 14, Gillmore was on Folly Island, whereupon he discovered that Du Pont would be replaced by Admiral Dahlgren. Both Dahlgren and Gillmore agreed with the War Board that "the navy would find it a comparatively easy task to ascend the harbor to Charleston." For his part, General Gillmore felt that the operation would first entail "the occupation of the southern portion of Morris Island; secondly, the capture of Wagner and Gregg; thirdly, the reduction of Sumter. With the reduction of Sumter the navy was to advance." Gillmore would alter this only in that he would reduce Fort Sumter before capturing Wagner and Gregg since Sumter was considered by both the army and navy to be the chief obstacle in taking Charleston.[95]

Meanwhile in Charleston Harbor, Confederate engineers began assessing the damage caused by the gunboats. Major William H. Echols reported a full account of the action and sent several drawings of the eastern and northeastern fronts depicting the shot marks received in the attack. Major General Gustavus W. Smith, acting then on General Beauregard's staff, visited the fort and reported that "the efficiency of the fort was not impaired by the recent bombardment." The report found that the "powerful shocks given by these projectiles to the solid masonry of the fort was something new" and "at the moment of impact, the loosening, shattering effects attending the shock exceeded all expectations." Thirty-four shots pockmarked the seaside fronts. Craters in the wall caused by more than one projectile were more serious, one measuring 2.7 feet in depth, 6 feet in height and 8 feet in width. The shelling damaged four embrasures and destroyed two; a section of the parapet on the eastern flank was breached, exposing the gun behind it. To provide some relief to the garrison, two hundred men of the Forty-Sixth Georgia Volunteers were dispatched to Fort Sumter to make repairs.

Major Harris suggested that all seafront casemates, lower and upper, be filled with sand. Labor and sand were in short supply, and the northeastern face was not filled. Another important consideration was protecting the magazines, especially from the reverse fire coming from the Federal squadron. To remedy this weakness, the upper magazines were abandoned so that the arches of the lower magazines could be filled with sand and reinforced with a brick wall on the outside of the gorge. The work was completed within four weeks, and the labor and expense of these improvements would be, as an engineer would later recall, "entirely vindicated" when the Federal bombardment resumed in the following months.

The engineers were most concerned with strengthening the parapet and protecting the fort's guns. While sand could be used to fortify the casemates from artillery fire, the Confederates needed to keep the interior of the parapet clear to ensure the effectiveness of the guns. The engineers also tried to suspend compressed bales of cotton, soaked in saltwater, over the exterior of the parapet by ropes and eyebolts drilled into the masonry. They hoped the arrangement could protect the brickwork from the powerful Union ordnance. But when guns were fired from Sumter, the cotton bales—dried from sun and wind exposure—burst into flames. Nothing went to waste in this time of war; the cotton bales were taken from the walls and used in the filling of the officers' quarters on the gorge "where, laid wet in sand, they did invaluable service by their bulk and resistance."

Among a smaller contingent of white mechanics and members of the garrison, 130 slaves were put to work "busily employed in unloading materials and various works of construction." The Confederate garrison was largely concerned with rearranging the fort's artillery to focus on any attack from Union ships. It needed to find larger artillery pieces, but aside from one eleven-inch gun salvaged from the *Keokuk*, Brigadier General Ripley and Colonel Rhett were unable to locate any artillery larger than that used in the fort's defense on April 7. All barbette guns of the western or left flank of the fort and those in the casemates were withdrawn from the fort and deployed in the inner harbor.

The parade ground was cluttered with plank ways, wheelbarrows and pits as slave laborers excavated sand to fortify the casemates and cover the magazines. The parade ground dropped a total of four feet and began to pool with saltwater at high tide as sand was excavated. To avoid fire from Union artillery, barges filled with sand were sent from Charleston each night to refill the parade ground and fill the casemates. Soon twelve lower and thirteen upper casemates on the seafront were protected by sandbags covered in tar.

To meet the demand, the engineer increased the number of laborers to 350 slaves working shifts day and night. One of the first tasks undertaken was to strengthen the gorge against land batteries. Though closed, the gorge was not as strongly built as other portions of Fort Sumter. Unless it was strengthened, the wall would be battered down, exposing the interior to artillery fire. To economize materials, bales of steam-compressed cotton soaked in salt water were given to the engineer "with orders that they should be laid in sand as bricks in mortar." The filling of the gorge proved to be the most laborious task undertaken for the defense of Fort Sumter in the summer of 1863. Beginning on July 20, seventeen rooms used for officers' quarters, eight lower and nine upper, were filled in less than three weeks. One room was left unfilled so that the space of the sally port could be reserved for future use.

The enemy approaching, it was determined that a new wharf and sally port needed to be constructed at a position that received defilation from direct enemy fire. One of the casemates on the western, or city-facing side, near the northwestern angle of the fort "was devoted to the purpose; the tedious work of enlarging the embrasure to the dimensions of a gateway was begun, and steps were taken to build a timber wharf projecting about fifty yards from the exterior of the fort into deep water. This double work, begun July 16th, was completed in nine days." It would prove an invaluable improvement as Fort Sumter would remain dependent on munitions, materials and men delivered via that wharf for the remainder of the war.[96]

As the Confederates strengthen Fort Sumter, General Gillmore was busy at work. During the summer of 1863, Union troops were constructing fortifications at the northern end of Folly Island under the watchful eyes of the Confederates. The precise nature of the works was hidden from view of the Confederates by "the formation of the island, covered with ridges of sandhills" and "dense jungle." Though the Confederates knew of the batteries, there were other positions on nearby James Island to worry General Beauregard.[97]

The Battle for Morris Island

On July 10, 1863, the concentrated fire of forty-seven guns from the hidden Federal batteries on Little Folly Island and eight-, eleven- and fifteen-inch guns in the monitors opened fire on Fort Wagner. As the iron raked the Confederate works, Union troops made a strong demonstration against James Island via the Stono River. These troop movements were intended as decoys, but Beauregard stated that they were made with "such strength that at any moment it could have been converted into a real attack of the most disastrous kind to us." Beauregard knew an attack on Morris Island was imminent but lacked the men to defend it and James Island. For the general, James Island was the key to Charleston's defense. If it fell, Federal guns would be brought up along the banks of the Ashley River and fired vertically through the city, the iron shells passing through house after house, day after day, until the city was razed to the ground.[98]

After battering the Confederates for three hours, the Federal guns fell silent, and 2,500 Union troops loaded into rowboats to cross Lighthouse Inlet. When Lieutenant Elbridge Copp of the Third New Hampshire Infantry was informed of the plan to capture Morris Island, he recollected that "cold shivers ran down my back, well knowing something of the horrors of facing a combined artillery and musketry fire under the most favorable circumstances, but to advance in open boats against the hail of grape and cannister, and a

Bomb and splinter proof of General Gillmore's works on Folly Island, South Carolina.

whirlwind of lead and exploding shell, called for the courage born either of reckless disregard for life or a martyr's duty to his God and country."[99]

After the Union guns went silent, the Confederates emerged from their foxholes and were drinking coffee in their encampments when they realized the Blue Backs were on the move. Their artillery was turned on the boats as they crossed the Folly River, and the Union troops were now rowing for their lives. Lieutenant Copp remembered the "zip and ping of the rebel bullets now singing about our ears, striking our boats, sometimes men…A shell explodes in the boat next to my own, killing and wounding many. The boat sinks, leaving a struggling mass of human forms in the water, reddened with the blood of the dead and wounded."[100]

Twenty-two-year-old Private John Weigel with the Seventy-Sixth Pennsylvania saw one of the Union boats cut in half by a Confederate shell, which also took off one of the legs of the men. He and the other men jumped into pluff mud and water up to their chests before storming the Confederate rifle pits, taking 150 prisoners and eleven pieces of artillery. Amid the fighting, he saw General Strong, leader of the amphibious assault, walking among the rifle pits, with "bare head, minus one boot, and in his shirt sleeves, pointing toward the rebel fort and shouting, 'Come on boys, the day is ours!'"

Meanwhile, the ironclads moved up Morris Island to keep Battery Wagner occupied and force the Confederates to abandon their artillery. The Rebels

focused on Admiral Dahlgren's flagship, the *Catskill,* and began to blaze
away. Although the artillerists managed to hit the vessel sixty times, they soon
discovered their guns were impotent against the ship's heavy armor with one
officer of the First Georgia Infantry recalling, "Again and again I saw the
solid ten-inch shot strike upon the sides of the monitors, only to break into
a thousand fragments, that splash into the sea like so much grapeshot."[101]

With their rifle pits and gun emplacements overrun, the Rebels fell back,
allowing the Union troops to move up Morris Island almost unopposed. Fort
Sumter continued to fire over Wagner, skipping its shells along the beach, which,
according to one soldier, "caused every man to have his eyes fixed toward the
fort." With the Union squadron providing covering fire, they pushed on, and

Battery B of the last U.S. artillery active during siege operations against Fort Wagner and Battery Gregg on Morris Island, South Carolina.

within a single day, the Blue Backs secured three-quarters of the island. Battery Wagner and Cummings Point might have been overrun, too, but it was hot as hell, and around 9:00 a.m., the Federal troops began to lose their momentum as the morning sun took its toll. "Many of our men were lying dead and wounded in front of the rifle pits and all along the line of march many were prostrated by the intense heat," recalled Elbridge Copp. After retreating behind a sand dune, he and a group of officers were enjoying a little butter and hardtack found in a Confederate tent when "a shell came plowing over the sands, bounding and striking within a few feet of us, nearly burying the whole party with dirt and demolishing our pail of butter, striking Colonel Bebel upon the leg as he sat upon the ground, wheeling him around and over and over like a tenpin." Covered

Haas & Peale.

with sand, the colonel jumped to his feet and yelled, "Where in H——ll is our butter?" An instant later, he saw the unexploded shell smoldering in the sand and threw it in the water. The fight was effectively over for the day, and Gillmore allowed his men to rest for an assault on Wagner the next day. Casualties were 294 Confederates and 107 Union soldiers dead, wounded and missing.[102]

On June 11, Union troops would make their first assault on Wagner. It was a far tougher undertaking than Gillmore anticipated. Originally constructed as a battery, Wagner was a now a formidable fortification protected by thirty-foot ramparts buffered by a water-filled ditch ten feet wide and five feet deep.

A photograph of Battery Hays taken by the team of Philip Haas and Washington Peale on Morris and Folly Islands during the summer of 1863.

Between the parapets and ditch were buried land mines and sharpened palmetto stakes. Because the battery was located at the northern end of Cummings Point, with the Atlantic on the east and a salt marsh on the west, it couldn't be flanked. The Union soldiers would have to rush slam-bang, head down into the teeth of the defenses, including heavy artillery, howitzers loaded with canister and grape and small arms of all kinds.[103]

The first attack on Wagner started at daybreak. After running headlong into Confederate fire, the Union troops broke in less than half an hour and retreated behind the dunes out of range of the Confederate batteries. A few of the soldiers managed to make it to the scarp of the work before realizing they were alone. Seeing they were unsupported, they laid down their weapons. One fellow had no such intentions and answered the call to throw down his rifle by climbing the parapet immediately in front of a thirty-two-pounder double charged with grape and firing at the officer in command, Lieutenant Gilchrist of South Carolina. All that the Confederates saw after the gun was fired was the "blue and mangled body" thrown over the ditch. The Confederates sustained twenty-four casualties; four hundred Union troops were listed as dead, wounded or missing.

After the rout, General Gillmore rethought his approach and ordered the construction of heavy batteries (Battery Reynolds, Battery Weed, Battery Hays and Battery O'Rourke) on Morris Island from 1,300 to 1,900 yards in front of Battery Wagner. These works would give the Federal armies cover in the planned assault on Battery Wagner.[104]

By July 17, the 460 men of the Federal camp were edging closer to Wagner. Alvin C. Voris, a lawyer from Akron who was now serving as a colonel with the Sixty-seventh Ohio Infantry, was stretched out on the sand a short distance from the fort. He and the men worked day and night, twelve hours on and twelve hours off, "all the while under shot and exploding shell from some quarter." At daybreak, he allowed the men to rest, reporting:

> Our poor tired bodies became so exhausted under the great pressure upon us, that we would stretch out on the burning sands, even when under the greatest danger, and snatch a few hours of fitful, anxious sleep, that vainly struggled to refresh us, frequently to be awakened by the explosion of some great shell, louder than the report of a ten pounder, scattering its fragments among the men commissioned with dismay and death. The land and sea breezes, for about one-half the time each day, kept the air full of floating sand, which permeated every thing—clothing, eyes, ears, nostrils,—and, at the height of the wind, would fly with such force as to make the face and hands sting with pain.

The next morning, on July 18, 1863, the Federals began a barrage on Fort Wagner with fifteen large mortars and twenty-five guns that dismounted cannons and blasted wooden barracks and storehouses to splinters. The guns were soon joined by Admiral Dahlgren's fleet. From the walls of Fort Sumter, Colonel Rhett estimated twenty-seven shells fell on Wagner per minute. Luther G. Billings, observing from a gunboat off Morris Island, recalled that the fire was kept up "until it seemed as if there could be nothing alive in the shapeless heap of sand which we had been so persistently battering." General

William B. Taliaferro, a forty-year-old Virginian and veteran of Stonewall Jackson's campaigns, commanded the Confederate garrison. Taliaferro knew a land assault would follow the shelling and gave Lieutenant Colonel P.C. Gaillard's Charleston Battalion the task of manning the ramparts during the barrage as lookouts. Inside the bombproofs, two North Carolina units, two companies of Georgia men and the First South Carolina Infantry waited for the spearhead of the Federal attack.[105]

After an eleven-hour bombardment that ended in a crescendo of artillery fire, Union armies moved on Battery Wagner at twilight, timed so the move wouldn't be seen from James Island, Sullivan's Island or Fort Sumter.[106] Bayonets fixed, the Fifty-fourth Massachusetts, commanded by Colonel Robert Gould Shaw, led the charge down the narrow beach. After sustaining fire from Wagner, Moultrie and Sumter, Captain John W.M. Appleton of the Fifty-fourth recollected, "At last we reached the moat of the fort. The sky had become black w/ clouds & the thunder cracked & lightening flashed... the tier cannonade in the bastions at that instant were fired; the one on the right tearing the right of the company to pieces, killing Sgt. Beton & others & almost at the same instant, a like disaster fell upon the left of the company from the bastion on the left." Watching from the deck of the USS *Water Witch*, Luther Billings recalled that the dead and dying were littered along the beach and that the "sand in front of the fort was so thickly strewn with blue that it seemed to be one solid color."[107]

A photograph of General Quincy A. Gillmore in front of his tent on Morris Island.

A photograph of Battery Reynolds showing mortars aimed at Wagner.

Despite being hammered by canister and rifle fire, the remnants of the Fifty-fourth crossed the ditch and began climbing the parapet. It was a wild, confused action fought in the midst of smoke, flying sand, the deafening retort of howitzers and the cries of dying men. Sergeant William Carney, who was shot in the hip during the assault, later recalled, "I had held for quite a while, and finding myself to be the only struggling man, as all around me, under me, and beside me, were dead or dying and wounded." After being mauled by a massive Confederate salvo unleashed when they reached the top of the parapet, the remnants of the Fifty-fourth broke and stumbled toward the rear.[108]

Haas & Peale

The parapet was littered with twisted and exploded corpses, yet the unwounded pushed ahead in what had to seem like slow-motion suicide. Colonel Haldimand S. Putnam, a West Point graduate of the class of 1857, would lead a four-regiment brigade in the second wave of the assault. He didn't pull punches before leading his men into the fight, telling his officers, "We are all going into Wagner like a flock of sheep." Colonel Putnam was soon dead, shot in the head. The Sixth Connecticut and Forty-eighth New York fought their way across Wagner's moat, briefly taking the southeastern bastion after a hand-to-hand fight with the Thirty-first North Carolina, which initially refused to leave the bombproof after the shelling ended. Just as the Sixth's color-bearer tried to plant the flag, he was shot down. Next up was the Seventh New Hampshire, which passed the Fifty-fourth as it moved to the rear. The Seventh found Wagner's ditch littered with the bodies of the dead and dying and was struck by shot and shell that, as one survivor reported, "seemed to fill the air like drops of rain."

The 100th New York, having ignored the order to remove the caps from their rifles and fight with bayonets alone, became confused and fired into the 3rd New Hampshire and 48th New York as they reached the top of the parapet. The men rolled back down the sandy embankment, many drowning in the ditch below. Others suffocated when fellow soldiers fell on them after the Confederate howitzers swept the ditch. Yet they pushed on. Troops from the 67th Ohio charged the fort and seized a Confederate artillery piece after a desperate fight with the gunners. Colonel Alvin Voris recalled, "I shudder as I think of that awful charge. I could hear the sickening thud of case and canister shot slashing through the bodies of men. How it was possible for a man to reach that fort alive is beyond my comprehension."[109] At this point, control of Wagner hung in the balance as Federal troops occupied a good portion of the fort; but when the Confederates were reinforced with the 32nd Georgia, the Yankee troops were surrounded and cut off. It took most of the night to eliminate the stragglers trapped inside Wagner. Those who managed to escape discovered a group of drunken Union artillerists tasked with stopping a retreat slashing men with their swords as they staggered to the rear.

At daybreak the Confederates began surveying the corpse-strewn battlefield and found the parapet and ditch littered with bodies. From all directions, men could be heard calling to their enemies for water, and one observer reported that "entreaties of the wounded the next morning, particularly the poor misguided negroes, was piteous." A Confederate writing to his family after the battle recalled:

> I never saw such a sight as presented itself on Sunday morning at day brake [sic]—as far as the eye could reach could be seen the dead and dying on all sides could be seen the result of the fight. I volunteered to go out to collect the wounded Yankees…I never saw such a sight, men with heads off many with legs shot off—feet, hands and in fact any part of the body—Such complete destruction of life—So wholesale—it makes me shudder to think of it.

The Confederates piled the dead into mass graves, with Shaw buried among his own troops. The injured were taken for treatment to Charleston, where the amputated limbs were stacked like cordwood at the door of the hospital. Total casualties were 1,689 (U.S.:1,515; C.S.: 174).[110]

After the assault on Battery Wagner, Lewis Douglass, the son of abolitionist Frederick Douglass, found time to write his fiancée, Amelia Loguen. He wanted her to know he was still alive but couldn't help but express his pride in his fellow soldiers: "My Dear Amelia: I have been in two fights, and am unhurt. I am about to go in another I believe to-night. Our men fought well on both occasions. The last was desperate—we charged that terrible battery on Morris Island known as Fort Wagoner [sic], and were repulsed with a loss of 300 killed and wounded. I escaped unhurt from amidst that perfect hail of shot and shell. It was terrible."[111]

Despite the high casualties, General Gillmore had no intention of giving up the offensive, and an offensive was exactly what Washington expected. Even while the bodies were being tallied, the general was devising a new strategy to take Fort Wagner. His plan was to take the slower, safer combination of bombardment from afar and slow encroachment to the Confederate works. In this phase of the campaign, the Union military employed new techniques such as trench warfare and continuous bombardment with artillery fire from the land coupled with gunboat attack from the sea. Gillmore's difficulty in this approach was the shifting nature of the soil and the field of decomposing corpses that the sappers had to dig through. His right flank was protected by the ironclads and his left by an impassable marsh, exposed only to the fire of batteries on James Island two and one-quarter miles distant. While a series of trenches was dug to Battery Wagner, soldiers were

A photograph of the Union Camp on Morris Island during the summer of 1863.

working under the protection of cannon fire and were ever vigilant of Confederate snipers.[112]

Determined to share the glory of taking Morris Island, Dahlgren was drawing up his own plans for Wagner. His idea was to land marines under the command of Major Jacob Zeilin in an assault from the Atlantic while the army moved in from the south. To his surprise, Zeilin advised Dahlgren against using marines in the attack on Fort Wagner. The marines were "incompetent to the duty assigned [them]," he reported, adding, "Sufficient sacrifice of life has already been made during this war, in unsuccessful storming parties, to make me anxious at least to remove responsibility from myself." The major argued that many of his

Two eight-inch Parrot rifles directed at Fort Sumter by Federal troops on Morris Island.

men lacked combat experience and that the hot South Carolina summer prevented training, "and no duty which they could be called upon to perform requires such perfect discipline and drill as landing under fire." Frustrated, Dahlgren was forced to abandon his plan, writing in his diary, "The Commander of Marines reports against risking his men in attacking [enemy] works…What are Marines for?"[113]

Meanwhile, during the summer of 1863, Gillmore's men were constructing fortifications at the northern end of Folly Island, and new works were pressed to completion on Morris Island for the mounting of breaching artillery for the reduction of Fort Sumter. On July 23, a gun was in place 4,200 yards away, and everyone knew that an artillery siege was imminent.

5
REQUIEM OF THE SHELL

For Quincy Gillmore, there was never any doubt what was in the cards for Fort Sumter. When he was charged with taking Fort Pulaski in 1862, he was warned by General Totten that, with the fort's seven-and-a-half-foot solid brick walls backed with stout masonry piers, "you might as well bombard the Rocky Mountains." Gillmore entertained no such doubts, and on the morning of April 10, he cut loose with thirty-six pieces from Tybee Island. After two days' work, Fort Pulaski was in ruins, and the Confederates hauled down their flag and called it a day.

Looking at Fort Sumter sitting off Morris Island, Gillmore was confident that the blueprint provided by Pulaski could be neatly applied to Sumter. In late July 1863, he directed his artillerists to begin throwing shells at Sumter to sight his guns and see how the individual shots registered on the fort's brick walls. Pleased with the results, on the morning of August 17, he ordered the Federal troops to open fire on Fort Sumter with land-based eight-inch Parrott guns. Sitting off Morris Island, Dahlgren watched the shells crash into the walls of Sumter. The firing commenced, he ordered the Federal squadron forward, leading with the *Weehawken*, followed by the *Catskill*, *Nahant* and *Montauk*. The *Passaic* and *Patapsco* were kept in reserve to attack Sumter, while the *Ironsides* was put in position to attack Wagner. As the tide pushed in, the *Weehawken* drew to within 450 yards of Fort Wagner and was followed by the other three monitors. The *Ironsides* was also brought up but, owing to its deep draught, was unable to engage at close range.

A view of Battery Rosecrans armed with three one-hundred-pounder Parrot rifles.

About 9:30 a.m., the guns of Fort Wagner fell silent and the *Passaic* and *Patapsco* ran up the channel within two thousand yards of Sumter and started whacking away at the fort's gorge and southeast walls with their rifled guns. With Fort Sumter incapable of responding with anything more than the eleven-inch gun salvaged from the *Keokuk* and Wagner silenced, at noon Dahlgren decided to pull back and allow his men to eat lunch. Content with the damage done to the fort's walls that morning, only the *Passaic* and *Patapsco* were sent back into action with orders to harass the Confederates if they tried to repair damage to Wagner. The success of that morning's action was tempered by the loss of two members of the Federal fleet. Among the dead was Dahlgren's chief of staff and friend Captain George W. Rogers, killed when the *Catskill* was hit by fire from Wagner.

On the night of August 17, the bombing of Sumter began in earnest and lasted for five days. Heavy siege batteries armed with English Whitworth rifles captured from the Confederates worked in conjunction with the gunboats to shower the fort with iron. Horatio Wait, serving aboard the USS *Pembina*, wrote of the bombardment: "At night it made the most wonderful display of pyrotechnics that I ever saw. The air was filled with the luminous curves and flashes of the projectiles. A fifteen-inch gun, when fired with a cored shot, produces such a concussion of the air as to make it unpleasant to the ears of those near it; and when this continues for a week, those firing are as glad of cessation as those fired at."[114]

Rear Admiral John A. Dahlgren standing by a Dahlgren gun.

In the first twenty-four hours of the bombardment, more than a thousand shells were fired on Fort Sumter. At dawn on the eighteenth, the bombardment continued with three additional guns joining in the fight. The gorge face and left face in reverse received the severest punishment, more guns were knocked out of action and the garrison flag was hit twice. All totaled, only 886 shots were fired on the second day because an abnormally high tide flooded the batteries, forcing a cessation in the bombing.[115]

As the fire tapered off, Confederate engineers began reviewing the damage and discovered crumbling masonry and a huge vertical crack running up the western wall caused by the concussion of shells striking the fort. After the inspection, it was feared Sumter's fall was imminent, and all material, ammunition and stores that could be spared were taken to Sullivan's Island while the two forty-two-pound guns were lowered to the parade for shipment to James Island. Because the fort was still taking harassing fire the night of the seventeenth, fatigue parties worked in shifts, stacking 1,500 bags of sand over and within the magazines and protecting the lower casemates on the western side with sandbags to allow it to serve as a hospital.

On the morning of August 20, the Federal guns opened on Fort Sumter at nine o'clock. It took five shots to find the range, but an officer with the Seventh Connecticut Infantry reported that it struck "with tremendous effect…throwing up great clouds of dust and brick high in the air." Federal troops working in the heat and humidity took a break to watch the show. All along the line, they cheered the destruction as the Confederates tried to knock the gun out of action. The firing continued throughout the day. The upper and lower casemates of Sumter were damaged, and the demolishing of the piers had already caused one of the upper arches to fall, uncovering the inside face of the scarp wall. The western barracks were in ruin and the spiral staircase wrecked. Two valuable ten-inch columbiads were also knocked out of action.

The next morning, the Federal firing resumed on Fort Sumter, but on the sixth shot, one of the guns exploded and had to be repaired using a makeshift forge inside the battery. Within twenty-four hours, the mechanics made the artillery piece ready, as one Union enlisted man would write, "to send its compliments to Fort Sumter in the shape of 300 pounds of iron."

It was at this time that Gillmore sent word to Beauregard that Fort Sumter and Morris Island were to be surrendered or he would turn his guns on the city. After Beauregard, who was off on other business, failed to respond, Lieutenant Charles Sellmer with the Eleventh Maine Infantry opened up at 1:30 a.m. with an eight-inch Parrot rifle called the "Swamp Angel." Working off a compass reading on St. Michael's steeple, the first shell, loaded with "Greek Fire," the Civil War equivalent of napalm, traveled 7,900 yards before falling into Charleston. Unable to sleep because of the heat, war correspondent Frank Vizetelly was reading *Les Misérables* in bed at the Charleston Hotel when he heard a crash, followed by a deafening explosion on the street. He could see fire from his window and rushed into the hall, where he found the terrified residents of the hotel scampering around in various stages of undress. He couldn't help but laugh when he saw that "one perspiring individual, of portly dimensions, was trotting to and fro with one boot on and the other in his hand, and this was nearly all the dress he could boast of." He wrote that the people were cursing the Federal commanders when another shell landed nearby, and "down on their faces every man of them [went] in tobacco juice and cigar ends and clattering among the spittoons." Another resident of the city, C.R. Buckmyer, recounted in a letter to his wife that one shell "entered the house directly opposite us… and commencing at the back garret had descended to the side walk through the house, passing through both floors and penetrating the walls as though they were paste board." Though no one was hurt by the "Yankee malignity," Burckmyer wrote that he and his neighbors "scattered and in two minutes not a soul was left in the lately crowded street."

Beauregard was furious and fired off a letter to his Federal counterpart stating, "It would appear, Sir, that…you have turned to the novel measure of turning your guns against the old men, the women and children, and the hospitals of a sleeping city—an act of inexcusable barbarity from your own confessed point of sight, inasmuch as you allege that the complete demolition of Fort Sumter within a few hours by your guns seems to you 'a matter of certainty.'" After the admonishing, Gillmore gave a brief reprieve for the Confederates to evacuate the city.

Though the 16,500-pound Swamp Angel exploded on its thirty-sixth shot, Gillmore found other guns to turn on Charleston. Wealthier families left the city for the interior towns of Columbia and Camden. The poorer residents were forced to live in makeshift shelters among the soldiers camped at the race course and other open spaces. Business and public institutions moved north of Calhoun Street out of range of the guns. For 587 days, the bombardment continued, fatiguing the city's residents and destroying morale. The days of grand parties were over, and one resident lamented in his diary that the city's prospects "grow darker and darker every day."[116]

On the morning of August 22, the monitors moved up and began ripping into Fort Sumter with their eleven- and fifteen-inch guns. The Confederate guns on Sullivan's Island and Battery Gregg responded to the shelling with their own artillery, but Fort Sumter was able to get off six shots. The fort's walls fronting the Atlantic were taking serious punishment and began to give way. Meanwhile, Gillmore's artillery continued to fire from Morris Island, and the seven-inch Brooke rifle at the southeastern angle was knocked out along with a ten-inch columbiad and a rifled and banded forty-two-pounder. At that moment, Sumter had only four serviceable guns and had lost the ability to command the ship channel or provide fire on the Union sappers working their way up Morris Island. The day's bombardment had seen a total of 604 shots, of which 203 struck outside, about an equal number landed inside and 183 passed over the fort. Though no one was killed or

A view of East Battery with a dismantled Blakely gun in the foreground.

seriously injured, one shot penetrated the floor of the upper tier, masonry collapsed and Colonel Rhett was cut by his own knife when the bricks fell on the table where he and his officers were eating. As Rhett was being patched up, the garrison was put to work repairing the merlons and traverses of the eastern or right flank, which had been damaged by the day's shelling.

On August 24, Brigadier General Gillmore reported to the War Department that 5,009 shells weighing in excess of half a million pounds had been fired on the fort and that Sumter was "a shapeless and harmless mass of ruins." Quoting his chief of artillery, Colonel J.N. Turner, Gillmore wrote that Fort Sumter was an "infantry outpost...incapable of annoying our approaches to Fort Wagner or inflicting injury upon the iron-clads." Nevertheless, the *New York Herald* reported that the "bombardment was going on with great energy, and the firing was very rapid." Sumter could no longer return fire and was described as "entirely demolished."[117]

Still there would be no surrender. On August 26, General Beauregard sent word to Rhett that Sumter, even in "its present shattered condition," was to be held "to the last extremity." The next day Brigadier General Roswell S. Ripley was instructed to reduce the garrison of Fort Sumter to a force of one company of artillery and two full companies of infantry, "not to exceed three hundred or fall below two hundred men."

"Of course you will select the companies, which must be of the best in your command of both arms; but it has been suggested that Captain Harleston's company of the First Regiment of Artillery would be suitable. The infantry should be carefully selected, and might be relieved once a week," wrote Thomas Jordan, chief of staff for Beauregard. Since the garrison's numbers were sharply reduced, Colonel Rhett moved his headquarters to Fort Johnson and Major Stephen Elliott was assigned the command of Fort Sumter.

At about 11:15 on the night of September 1, bright flashes followed by the reports from the guns at Sullivan's Island announced to the city that the Federal gunboats were on the move. Colonel Rhett sent a dispatch to General Ripley's headquarters stating that six monitors were closing on Sumter. By this time, Moultrie and most of the other batteries on Sullivan's Island were mixing it up with the gunboats. Meanwhile, Battery Gregg, at Cummings Point, was put on alert and told to be prepared should the ironclads try to run the gauntlet into the harbor. Soon the gunboats were blazing away and the *Charleston Mercury* reported that Fort Sumter "alone stood grimly silent throughout the ordeal to which she was exposed, and the dark outline of her parapet was lit up only by the frequent flashes of the enemy shells as they burst above her shattered walls."

Regarding the action, the *Mercury* reported:

The scene was one not to be forgotten. The moon shone brightly from an almost cloudless sky, lighting up the whole expanse of our beautiful harbor, and rendering Batteries Bee and Gregg, with the entervening [sic] forts, distinctly visible along the misty horizon. Every moment the broad flashes of the guns could be seen, now far away on the extreme right, where the Yankee land batteries kept pounding away at Battery Wagner, now on the left, from Moultrie or the batteries near by, and anon, at regular intervals of six minutes, from each of the monitors, which seemed to be drawn up in line of battle just off Sumter, but at what distance we could not determine with any degree of accuracy.

The paper reported that at 4:00 a.m., the gunboats were "still pegging away [at] the stately and still defiant Ruin." The next morning, Union soldiers, relieved to get a break from the heavy booming of the artillery, celebrated when Dahlgren and Gillmore decided that the masonry of Sumter's gorge wall was sufficiently wrecked to let their guns go silent.

If the garrison at Fort Sumter was suffering from the Union artillery, the troops at Battery Wagner had it worse—much worse. Day after day, the gunboats and batteries blazed away while sappers inched closer to the southeastern corner of the fort. The thunder of artillery was a deafening constant, and even the night afforded no relief. One witness reported that "as the night advanced the discharge of artillery became more frequent. A more beautiful pyrotechnic display was never seen. Balls of fire from the rockets crossed each other in the heavens above the neutral ground and fell bursting with a shower of brilliant sparks into the works."[118]

The fall of Wagner was now a certainty. All that could be done was bleed the Yankees until they finally took the fort. In the meantime, both sides had to see it through with all the suffering and death that it might require. It was hell. Private Theodore A. Honor with the Twenty-fifth Carolina Infantry wrote to his fiancée that the sentinels posted outside during the bombardment suffered the worst casualties. "For Thirty six hours three surgeons did nothing but amputate limbs or dress wounds or pass sentence of death upon the poor fellows," he wrote. Suffering from a bout of dysentery in Wagner's hospital, he saw friend after friend hauled in dead or with arms or legs gone. Corporal Augustine Smythe with the C.S. Signal Corps later wrote of his time at Wagner: "The water was putrid, corpses buried in the sand hills around were torn up by the shell & exposed to the sun, the sick and wounded were unable to be cared for in place where a sound man could scarcely care for himself." The siege was drawing to a close by late summer. William Stryker recalled the 11,500 Union soldiers, "white and black, had labored with all the zeal and all the strength they possessed and not a murmur had escaped from the worn-out soldiery. Many were sick! The heat was intense and very unnerving, yet the goal was near and every one kept up a good heart and cheered each other as they labored in the batteries at rifle pits, exposed to shot and shell." Those that failed to keep their head down could expect to catch a sniper's bullet. "Every angle of the approaches, every opening in the parapets, every loop hole almost, was covered by the sharp-shooters, and the singing of the minie balls was

A map of Gillmore's position on Morris Island during the bombardment of Sumter.

like the music of immense mosquitoes," recalled Lieutenant William Furness of the Third U.S. Colored Troops.[119]

On September 6, 1863, Union sappers reached the ditch in front of Wagner. There was nothing left to be done. The Confederates evacuated both Battery Wagner and Battery Gregg on September 7, and Federal forces entered Wagner without a fight. Elbridge Copp said that upon entering the fort, they discovered the Confederates tossed their dead over the parapet where they rolled into a ditch on the outside. They found bodies in piles, "the limbs and bodies swollen beyond the semblance of human form, with eyes protruding, faces distorted into an expression of fiends, the decomposition filling the air with stench intolerable, and beyond endurance—we seemed to have entered the very gates of hell."[120]

The day after the fall of Battery Wagner, Dahlgren sent word to the Confederates that Sumter was to surrender. Unimpressed, Stephen Elliott replied: "Inform Admiral Dahlgren that he may have Fort Sumter when he can take and hold it." Believing that the fort was only defended by a corporal's guard, the admiral had every intention of taking Elliott's challenge and was already preparing to storm Sumter that evening. Gillmore was determined to do the same and suggested a joint attack under his command. Dahlgren wasn't interested in sharing the glory with the general and ordered an immediate attack on the fort by five hundred marines and sailors in twenty-five small boats, led by Commander Thomas H. Stevens, USN.

After being towed into the harbor by the *Daffodil*, the rowboats were ordered to pull toward Sumter with utmost haste but in complete silence. Captain Charles G. McCawley, the senior marine in the night assault and another future commandant, recalled, "After much delay the boats were cast off [from the steam tug] and in great confusion; the strong tide separated them, and I found it quite impossible to get all my boats together."

The operation was a debacle from the start. The attacking force had no idea how many men were in the fort and they had no ladders to scale the crumbling walls. Operational security was also compromised. The Confederates, having captured a Union codebook earlier that summer, deciphered Dahlgren's signals and were preparing for the assault. The surrounding forts and batteries sighted their guns on Sumter's seaward approaches while the Confederate ironclad *Chicora* slipped in behind the fort.

The Confederate's held their fire until the landing party reached shore around midnight. Sentries fired a signal rocket, and all the batteries in the harbor opened fire with grape and shell. Only eleven of the twenty-five boats landed on the rocks beneath the fort; the others were either sunk by Confederate fire or forced to retreat into the dark. Those who managed to get onshore tried to rally and were greeted with a shower of rifle fire, bricks, hand grenades and Molotov cocktails tossed from above.

Suffering a withering crossfire and seeing dozens of their comrades slain, the surviving 105 invaders laid down their arms and surrendered after only twenty minutes of action. Found in their possession were libations for a victory celebration and five Union flags, one of which was the garrison flag that survivors believed was the one Major Anderson flew over Sumter in April 1861. The prisoners were conducted to a casemate in the western face where Stephen Elliott reported they were "so delighted at not being shot that they were quite jolly at first but by breakfast time they seemed to realize their position more fully." His words proved prophetic. Lieutenant Meade would spend the next thirteen months of his life as a prisoner of war in Columbia, South Carolina, and was lucky to survive. Twenty-one marines taken at Fort Sumter that night would die as prisoners of war in Andersonville, Georgia.[121]

The Northern public was apoplectic, and it was now Dahlgren's turn to take a beating in the newspapers. After finally taking Morris Island with considerable loss of life, the admiral was entreated by the *New York Herald* to give up the ghost because there was no "actual necessity for possessing the ruins of Fort Sumter, or for taking notice of Fort Moultrie or any other fort on the northern margin of the harbor, beyond drawing their fire while other operations are in progress in order to capture and to hold the city of Charleston." It would appear that Fort Sumter was proving too tough a nut to crack, and with the repulse on September 8, the press continued to

This photograph shows the site of the failed night attack on Fort Sumter on September 8, 1863.

urge the military command to abandon the assault, arguing it "is surely not necessary for a man to run his head against a stone wall in order to enter a house when he can go in by the door."[122]

On September 28, another bombardment began. All day, the men in gray crowded into some safe corner and tried to get some rest. Two days into the barrage, Stephen Elliott retired to his quarters and wrote to his wife about life under siege:

This photograph shows Battery Gregg with the ruins of Fort Sumter in the distance.

I have come back to my old room that looks in comparison like a place, where I am undisturbed, except by having to give orders for moving the guns from the parapet. The moon has risen now and probabilities of barrages are lessened for the night. I am beginning to take things more quietly, the garrison is in good training and officers and men understand their duty and we will hammer them pretty seriously if they try it [amphibious attack]. I sleep over here at night—it is so much nicer than the other place which is close and dirty—the necessary attributes of "safety." The mosquitoes are perfectly awful and I have to smoke constantly tonight while writing to keep them from eating me up; my pipe is now out so I must build a smoke. So now the fire is built and I can be comfortable for a little while. I have a nice little mosquito net left here by somebody and get along first rate after I get to bed except in one very important particular which I will leave to your imagination to suggest.

As summer became fall and the days grew shorter and cooler, the Confederates hunkered down behind their shattered walls. Their guns were silent save a few shots thrown over to pester the Yankees. Meanwhile, on Morris Island, there was little to report on as the shadows grew longer. There was the occasional skirmish on James Island, but for the most part, the Federals busied themselves with improving their batteries and harassing their counterparts at Fort Sumter.[123]

6
THE STATELY AND STILL DEFIANT RUIN

Though fire on Fort Sumter was briefly suspended, on October 26, Federal troops observed new guns being mounted on the right flank wall, and another bombardment was carried out from Battery Gregg, now rebuilt, reoriented and renamed Fort Putnam. Later that day, the *Patapsco*, *Lehigh*, *Weehawken* and *Nahant* moved up opposite Fort Wagner and began pounding Sumter and "continued it leisurely during the day," while the eleven- and fifteen-inch guns of Morris Island "battered the walls in fine style." On Friday afternoon, the *New York Herald* reported that after the *Patapsco* and *Lehigh* took turns striking the southeast face of the fort, it "presented an appearance of demolition and ruin" that "resembled, at a distance, the ruins of some old Moorish castle…with the tattered, dirty rebel flag floating from a shattered rammer staff, on an obscure bastion, without a gun beneath it to utter a defiance or repel a foe."[124]

Though Moultrie, Bragg, Johnson and Simpkins tried to take the heat off the fort by throwing iron at the Yankees, fire was kept up day and night with murderous efficiency. Soon Sumter's eastern wall was reduced to a mass of debris, forming an inclined plane of about twenty-five degrees from the water to the top of the wall. It was remarkable anyone could survive the battering, and even the Union troops marveled at the tenacity of Sumter's garrison with one writing on the twenty-eighth that "the irrepressible 11th S.C. hold out."

Reporting from Battery Gregg on the morning of October 29, Corporal Henry Gooding, a soldier of the Fifty-fourth Massachusetts who was born

This photograph shows the parapet of Fort Sumter.

into slavery in North Carolina and would later die as a prisoner of war in Andersonville, Georgia, wrote that he could see "the sad havoc made on the once formidable Sumter." For upward of fifteen minutes, he reported, the fort was obscured by smoke "so rapid was the fall of shell, in and around it." At ten o'clock, the flag and staff were shot away and the Union troops rushed from their guns, pickets and fatigue parties to mount the parapets, waving their hats, caps and even shovels to observe this small victory. Their celebration was short lived. "Amid the shouts and rejoicings, the bellowing of guns, the whizzing of ponderous balls, and the bursting of bombs over that doomed citadel, another flag is raised out of the black smoke," recalled Gooding. With the flag flying again, the Confederate soldier coolly doffed his cap to the Union artillerists and ducked back into the fort. After watching this "trick," the corporal admitted "grave doubts of ever getting the rascals out."[125]

On October 30, a fierce bombardment was kept up all day on Sumter from the monitors and land batteries. Over 1,200 shots were fired in twenty-four hours, and it was reported that the "bricks on Fort Sumter flew in clouds." On October 31, a shell slammed into the fort barracks and buried thirteen soldiers sleeping there. Two more were killed and another four injured later that day during a mortar attack. That evening, a Union solider serving on Morris Island sent a letter to the *New Bedford Mercury* assuring its readers that "the way everything looks now is that Sumter must and shall fall."[126]

Living conditions in the fort were nightmarish. Even the usually stoic Stephen Elliott, who preferred to write about "the ♫ of parrott shells" and "fine whiskey" began to show signs of intense stress, writing to his wife, Charlotte, on Halloween night:

There I was at the end of the week all right in mind and body though I will own I was little blue this afternoon. The fact of having lots of stupid people to manage whose stupidity is chiefly attributable to fear and parcel of Georgian officers who have no more pride about obeying orders than Benjamin has and having to make out a post return and have all the command returns in and no muster rolls and an adjutant steeped in a mixture of hopeless melancholy and nauseous sycophancy and dead men being toted around the dinner table and men crushed, strangled beheaded and mangled being every now and then lugged in and every body looking at me as [if] I did it when if I had my way the old fort would be blown tonight in to as many pieces as there are bricks in it and then the constant arrival of some of the nine hundred and two visitors that have come over the sea and the constant sapping at "W" to which they have at last turned their attention and mixture of all sorts of people in my private apartment with out my having the power to drive them out and think. I have drawn a picture not by any means agreeable. Last night I placed sixteen men in a position convenient for mounting the parapet in one of the barracks and about 3 o'clock the roof knocked down by a shell and fell killing them all except one who was not sleepy and who was standing outside and got out of the way and two others not of the detachment making thirteen in all. I placed the men myself with some encouraging remarks as they would probably be the first engaged and really thought that they occupied the most desirable position of any men on duty. But we cannot always tell about these things. I do not blame myself a bit about it as I am perfectly conscious of having acted for the best. I feel quite hopeful and strong tonight. I expect you will doubt it after the tone my letter. [127]

Casualties continued to mount up over the next few days. One man was killed and another seven injured during a mortar attack on November 2. Four days later, a mortar plunged into a casemate, wounding fifteen men, three mortally. Given the week's losses, it's likely that one member of Sumter's garrison, William Hamilton Hayne, the son of Charleston poet Hamilton Hayne, took to heart his father's advice to "always despise…Yankees for they are bad, wicked, deceitful people." [128]

By November 7, the top of the wall downward to within ten or twelve feet from the base was knocked down, and it was reported that the "fort on that side [the seafront] presents the appearance of a regular sand work before it is sodded." This destruction did nothing to diminish the fort's defensive capacity, and as one Union soldier acknowledged, "Now, all the guns in Christendom can never effectually displace the debris accumulated there, for the more projectiles thrown into the mass, the stronger it becomes." Nonetheless, the shells continued to fly in, and a correspondent with the *New York Times* reported on November 9 that the "old fabric is gradually dropping away, revealing in the process portions of shattered casemates and other internal structure, which in turn disappear from view." Though he made no attempt to conceal his joy, the journalist did regret "that with its destruction perished the monument of valor and patriotism exhibited by a few noble men in the early stage of the rebellion." With Sumter now a ruin, he assured readers that the fort's demise was a foregone conclusion. Yet somehow, they held on. At sundown each night, to assure the people of Charleston that the garrison endured, a salute was fired to the Confederate flag as it was lowered for the evening. [129]

With Sumter's walls reduced to piles of rubble, Gillmore decided to test Sumter's defenses with an amphibious attack. There were a number of feints, and for weeks, the Federal troops were put on nightly alert. As one soldier reported, "It is 'reliably' reported daily, that such and such a regiment is to 'lead the charge on Sumter to-night.'" [130] After artillerists pounded the fort all day with the heavy Parrott rifles, on the evening of November 20, 1863,

Sketch of the entrance to Three Gun Battery at fort Sumter on December 9, 1863.

barges were filled with two hundred soldiers and headed for Fort Sumter. After they came under small arms fire about three hundred yards from the fort, the officers thought better of the attack and ordered the barges to turn around and retire to James Island.

Though the amphibious assault was called off, the artillery barrage continued unabated. The Union batteries kept up the fire "furious and incessant" for forty-one days, battering the fort's walls with fifteen thousand pounds of metal. Although the guns of Sumter were silent, the fort was far from defenseless. As the Federal guns leveled the walls of the fort, Confederate forces were constructing a new system of interior defenses that would turn the interior of the fort into a trap if the Union forces managed to breach the outer walls. It was determined that every inch of the interior parade and casemates would be contested by turning every casemate from which a view of the parade ground could be seen into a loophole for infantry fire. If the Federal troops stormed the fort, they would naturally end up at the center, where they would find the fort's garrison positioned above them. They also positioned a twelve-pound howitzer on a low arch near the northwestern angle that could sweep the parade with grape and canister. If Federal troops managed to get a foothold inside Sumter, the Confederates would duck into the bombproofs while their land-based batteries began a sustained bombardment on the fort to drive the Yankees out.[131]

By and large, the responsibility for making improvements to Fort Sumter fell to a workforce of one hundred slaves and ten white mechanics supervised by the engineer in charge. The slaves slept during the day and worked until sunrise. It was brutal. As the laborers and engineers worked, the fort was illuminated by the eerie calcium lights on Morris Island while mortars and Parrott shells were directed at the fort, killing and maiming indiscriminately. Between November 21 and 25, four slaves were killed by Federal fire, and another had a leg blown off. On the twenty-fourth, a Confederate officer was killed inspecting the infantry obstructions strung along the foot of the seawall. After this string of fatalities, it was decided to rotate out the laborers every two weeks.[132]

Materials were also brought in from the peninsula to hold the fort during the bombardment. This transfusion became so critical for the survival of Fort Sumter that Lieutenant Colonel Harris, chief engineer of the department, made it his top priority to ensure the steady supply of sand, tools and laborers to the fort daily. Unless the weather was too rough to hazard the crossing, barges and boats were dispatched to Fort Sumter every night, many taking beatings from Federal fire in the process. The Confederates were vigilant of amphibious attack, and if the ships failed to follow protocol, friendly fire was a near certainty. In one such incident, the steamer *Sumter* was relieving troops at Fort Wagner and failed to observe the communications signals used to prevent friendly fire on Confederate ships. As the *Sumter* drew nearer Fort Moultrie, a gun was fired and a signal sent up, but the captain made no response. Soon the ship was being targeted by the Confederate batteries, and it was reported that "shot and shell tore through the crowds of men on the steamer's deck."

The captain tried to alter course and run between Fort Sumter and James Island, but it was too late. Some men drowned, others were picked up by relief boats or stripped off their uniforms and swam to Fort Sumter. Colonel Charles Olmstead with the First Georgia Infantry recalled:

That night…I heard the sound of troops passing by and went out to find who they were. It proved to be a Regiment that had just been relieved from

A view of the interior of Fort Moultrie looking toward Fort Sumter.

duty at Fort Sumter and was on the march for the interior of the island. As the rear came there were the notes of a fiddle played by a soldier in gray, following whom was a singular procession of ghostly figures arrayed in white, dancing and frolicking like a lot of children. These were the men who swam to the fort from the wreck that morning; they had landed naked and been clad in hospital night-shirts, the only available clothing. All day they had endured the terrific fire that was rained upon Fort Sumter; yet here they were as I saw them.[133]

The firing on Fort Sumter was kept up through November, but still one Union soldier conceded that "the gallant rebels are masters of the situation."[134] By early December, the firing began to slacken, and with ammunition running low and the guns wearing out, by the sixth, the shelling stopped entirely.

On December 11, most of the work parties had just lain down to get some rest when the fort shuttered from a tremendous explosion. Although most powder had been removed from Sumter, about 150 pounds were stored in the lower western magazine. At 9:30 a.m., Captain Edward Frost was distributing rations there when the small arms magazine exploded, likely from a spark from his lantern. The explosion rushed into the adjoining commissary store, into the passage connecting the circular stair and the casemates of the western front and finally into the gallery leading out into the parade. The effects to the fort itself were immediate and profound. The explosion left a crater in the crest of the gorge around ten feet deep with the building material falling into the space below. Several arches also collapsed, and the fire was fed by materials stored in the commissary and ammunition cooking off in the magazines.

Inside the fort, there was the utmost confusion. The passageways were choked with dense smoke, forcing the garrison from the lower casemates where they found men fleeing the heat and stretcher parties rushing in the other direction to retrieve the injured. Shells burst overhead, and a dense blanket of smoke and brick dust darkened the morning sky. Through all the confusion, it was discovered that soldiers in the upper casemates were trapped by the heat and smoke. They were rescued through an opening that had been recently punched through a wall to serve as a gallery.[135]

Elliott rushed to the scene from his room in one of the lower casemates on the northwest flank. He recalled soberly, "I soon got round to the inside of the fort and seeing where the damage lay went through the passage heading back into our room near the magazine. To walk over dead and burning in your stocking feet is not very pleasant but que voulez vous?" He removed the injured and then reentered the magazine, where he found the fire had already destroyed the fort's provisions and was spreading at great speed. Eleven men were dead, many incinerated to ashes, and forty-one were wounded.[136]

Members of the First South Carolina under the command of Captain Alfred S. Gaillard began to pile bags of sand in the passage of the western casemates to block the fire, and all openings that could provide oxygen to the fire were blocked to suffocate the flames.[137] Their efforts were largely ineffectual. Within three hours of the explosion, the fire devoured everything in the upper casemates adjoining the southwestern angle and began to destroy the upper flight of wooden stairs and the bombproof timbers that covered and secured the stair tower. The fire also consumed the woodwork in the first tier to the howitzer platform in the casemate of the new sally port. From the magazine to the parade ground, the wooden gallery was effectively destroyed for half its length, the gates of the casemates were burned away and the bricks glowed white from the heat.[138] The lower casemates remained sealed, and water was used to cool them over two days until members of the garrison could get inside. They next entered the commissary room four days after the explosion where they discovered that sand caved in the roof and left ten feet of debris in the stair tower and passageways. It would take another ten days to enter the magazine. Due to the intense heat, the masonry of the magazines was brittle and falling away.[139]

The evening of the eleventh, one hundred men and more provisions were dispatched from Fort Johnson, a critical infusion of manpower and materiel. With their arrival, Elliott retired to his quarters and discovered that someone had made off with his best coat and pistols. Though his sword and books were still there, he wrote to his wife that once the emergency was under control, he would go to Charleston to be fitted for a new suit of clothes. Though he had been struck on the foot and head by falling bricks from the Union shelling, he assured his wife that they were "only shallow cuts on the lump on the back part of my skull which is thick."[140]

A few nights after the catastrophe, the fort was visited by General Beauregard, accompanied by Colonel Rhett and chief engineer Lieutenant Colonel Harris, for the purpose of inspection. Though the Yankees threw in over five hundred shells during the emergency, they didn't recognize the desperate situation the fort faced and the firing tapered off. This reprieve gave the Confederates time to evaluate the damage and after a review by the War Department, an all-out effort was made to rebuild the quarters and restore communications within the fort. The supply of labor and materials for construction were made a top priority, and it was decided that despite all the damage it sustained, Sumter would not be abandoned.

Morale in the Northern camp was nearly as gloomy as that of the Confederates as the year drew to a close. "The whole face of nature now presents a drear and gloomy appearance, and the thousands who a month or two ago were full of hope and expectation have gradually come down to that frame of mind so well adapted to wait till something turns up," wrote James Gooding from Morris Island. The fleet inside the bar was steadily reduced, and by the end of the month, only the monitors and the *Ironsides* were left together with three or four tugs and provision schooners.

The holidays provided a small break from the boredom, and on Christmas day, Gooding reported the troops enjoyed apple dumplings and rye whiskey as they watched the gunners give "the rebels in Charleston a Merry [or dismal] Christmas greeting, by throwing a few shell in among them." From

An illustration of South East Angle of Fort Sumter on December 9, 1863.

Morris Island, they could see oily black smoke rising from the city and reported that the "sound of the church bells could be distinctly heard…but whether it was the regular ringing of Christmas bells by the Catholic and established churches, or merely the alarm bells on account of fire, is difficult to determine." Even as he watched the city burn, Gooding conceded, "Christmas has come and gone, but Charleston still holds her head high, as the leading city in the van of the rebellion."[141]

Inside Fort Sumter, members of Company K, First South Carolina Artillery Regiment did the best with what they had. That afternoon, as their comrades battled Federal gunboats on Johns Island, they enjoyed Christmas with

> *an elegant dinner served on the chassis of a 10-inch Columbiad. For chairs to match this improvised table, the soldiers employed carpetbags, sandbags, stands of grape and round-shot from which to open an assault on a plentiful supply of roast turkey, wild duck, oysters, and sweet potatoes.*

The centerpiece in the headquarters casemate of the "Three Gun Battery" that day perfectly represented the spirit of the garrison. It was a half of a 15-inch shell, delivered presumably by a Yankee cannon, set in a flattened sandbag and serving for a punch bowl!

Winter provided the Confederates some relief, and they began to make improvements to Sumter in anticipation of a renewed spring attack. To open lines of communication between sections of the fort, engineers began to construct a labyrinth through the mass of rubble. First, a tunnel was dug through the ruins that lay between the sally port on the west and the three-gun battery on the east. They cut through solid masonry, gun carriages and every other kind of rubbish that had accumulated in the parade ground. The tunnel was three feet wide and six feet high and was fortified with heavy planks. Engineers also constructed a smaller fifty-foot tunnel by digging from the center bombproof through the basement rooms of the gorge to the abandoned southeastern magazine. Over the next month, they dug through wet sand and soaked cotton bales. Near the magazine, engineers had to break through a five-foot brick pier.[142]

With the battering of the eastern wall into rubble, debris had piled up on the outside of the fort and was being washed away by wave action. The loss of this rubble was a concern to engineers, who recognized that the mass provided protection to the eastern wall. To arrest the erosion, a series of iron girders, at one time used as floor joists, were set in the crevices of the rocks. They worked like a fence to secure the debris in a kind of permanent footing for the slope.[143] The girders served as an invaluable protection to the exposed flanks for the remaining years of the Confederate operation and also allowed engineers to stretch wire across the sloping debris to obstruct an assaulting enemy in a manner similar to barbwire.

On the night of January 28, Federal guns opened fire with heavy rifles and columbiads. The three-day bombardment was aimed at Fort Sumter's southeastern and southwestern angles. Firing was not resumed until March 10, when 143 shots were directed at the east angle of the fort. The three casemates in this section were lightly protected by their scarp wall, it having been damaged by earlier fire from the land batteries and naval ships. The wall had been fortified during the winter months by cribwork erected on the exterior of the fort. Engineers created the lower portion of the cribwork with pine timber and the upper sections with palmetto. The ten-foot-thick cribwork was then filled with ballast stone, brick and masonry debris found within the fort. Once its construction was discovered, the monitors signaled

A photograph of the Three Gun Battery taken at the end of the war.

to the batteries, which focused their artillery fire on the cribwork.[144] Though repeatedly struck, it was largely undamaged and stayed intact for the remainder of the war.

On March 2, 1864, Admiral Dahlgren's son, Ulrich, who had already lost a leg in a skirmish after the Battle of Gettysburg, was killed outside Richmond during a raid on the Confederate capital. The operation was ostensibly to rescue Union POWs, but found on Dahlgren's person were memos about the raid, including one document that stated, "The City it must be destroyed and Jeff Davis and Cabinet killed."

After the Confederates discovered the attempt to kill Jefferson Davis, they began to devise their own plans to bomb the White House and perhaps kill Lincoln. Among the alleged conspirators was the actor and Southern sympathizer John Wilkes Booth.

The Confederates were enraged. Within two weeks of the raid, they were devising their own plans to bomb the White House and perhaps kill Lincoln. Among the alleged conspirators was the actor and Southern sympathizer John Wilkes Booth. Meanwhile, Southern newspapers printed the Dahlgren memos, and it became an accepted fact across the Confederacy that Abraham Lincoln sanctioned the attempt to assassinate President Davis.

On April 20, 1864, Major General Samuel Jones arrived in Charleston to take command of the Department of South Carolina, Georgia and Florida from Beauregard. He found the eastern and southern sections of the city, now macabrely called the "Gillmore District," in ruins, with buildings gutted by fire and the streets chewed up by artillery fire. Jones, angered by what he saw, and no doubt aware of the attempt to kill Jefferson Davis and his cabinet, requested from the military command fifty Federal officers be rushed to Charleston to be "confined in parts of the city still occupied by civilians, but under the enemy's fire." Jefferson Davis approved the request, and prisoners from Camp Ogelthorpe in Macon, Georgia, arrived on June 12 by train. The *Mercury* was delighted at the news and reported to its readers, "These prisoners we understand will be furnished with comfortable quarters in that portion of the city most exposed to enemy fire. The commanding officer on Morris Island will be duly notified of the fact of their presence in the shelled district and if his batteries still continue at their wanton and barbarous work, it will be at the peril of the captive officers."[145]

On the night of May 4, 1864, Colonel Elliott was relieved of his command at Fort Sumter. Elliott had taken over command of Sumter—as the chief engineer described it, "a dismantled and silenced fort, a ruined habitation, an exposed outpost, a perilous command"—but he managed to hold the fort against great odds. His replacement was Captain John C. Mitchell of the First South Carolina Artillery, the son of Irish nationalist John Mitchell. After a forced exile to Australia, Mitchell immigrated to the United States in 1853 and threw in with the Confederacy with the outbreak of hostilities. There was as also a shakeup in the Federal command at this time. As Elliott left for his new assignment in Virginia, John G. Foster, now a major general, assumed command of the Department of the South. No one knew more about Sumter than Foster, as he had supervised its construction in the months and years leading up to the war.

7

THE PALE OF DEATH

Born fifty-six years before the man who is credited with the saying, John G. Foster could be forgiven for not knowing the axiom that "insanity is doing the same thing over and over again but expecting different results." Nevertheless, the major general should have known from the results of the previous eleven months that no amount of bombing was going to get the Confederates out of the ruins of Fort Sumter. Yet beginning on July 7, he tried just that. For eight weeks, Foster cut loose with everything he had, and no one, gray or blue, got a reprieve from the cannonading that thundered day and night.

To meet the challenge, the chief engineer at Fort Sumter, Captain John Johnson, requested a force of two hundred laborers and fifty mechanics and engineers to repair the damage. The fort was also chronically short of materials, and barges nightly visited Sumter to try to keep pace with the destruction.[146] To harass and kill laborers, the artillerists set the fuses of Parrott shells to explode directly above the fort, showering deadly fragments in every direction. Among those serving at Sumter was Milton M. Leverette, then serving as the fort's ordnance sergeant. When he arrived in May 1864, he wrote to his mother, "You needn't worry yourself…I expect a dull time."

By the end of May, after less than three weeks' service at Fort Sumter, Leverette was depressed in spirits and disillusionment crept into his correspondence. His dreams of heroism, he wrote to his mother, "turned like Dead Sea Apples to ashes on my lips." Save passing mention in the local papers, he believed the Confederacy's defenders could expect nothing more than to be left rotting on the ground. Though it was midday when he sat down to write, his quarters reminded him of a prisoner cell where the inmates go insane for want of sunlight. He promised to stay on at Sumter to satisfy is parents but wished only that he "could be on the cars rushing home, breathing the free air of heaven and being in its pure sunshine."

As the fort was shelled to pieces in the summer of 1864, the Confederates collected slaves from the countryside to repair the damage. Among those brought in was Jacob Stroyer, a slave born on Kensington Plantation in Eastover, South Carolina, and conducted at age fourteen with 364 other bondsmen to serve at Fort Sumter.

It was not Stroyer's first to trip to the Charleston Harbor. In the

John G. Foster, now a major general, assumed command of the Department of the South. No one knew more about Sumter than Foster, who had supervised its construction in the months and years leading up to the war.

summer of 1863 he was shipped by railcar along with several thousand slaves from across to the state to repair forts, build batteries and mount guns for the Confederates. While serving on Sullivan's Island, he witnessed a Confederate officer stab with a dirk between the collarbone and left shoulder a child serving as his body servant. He and the other laborers waited for the officer to be taken into custody for the murder but recalled that the authorities "treated it as coolly as though nothing had happened."

Compared to the labor on the plantation, Stroyer considered his two months' service on Sullivan's Island a relief and was sad to see it come to an end. A few slaves even managed to escape to the Union lines by swimming across to Isle of Palms, then called Long Island. Now back in Charleston a year later, Stroyer and the other bondmen waited to board steamers on Johns Island for a new assignment at Fort Sumter. The slaves being rotated out warned them that a fresh hell waited them in the harbor, not least because the fort's commanding officer, Captain Mitchell, was "harsh and cruel" and "sought every opportunity to expose the negroes to as much danger as he dared." Their observations proved prescient. After traveling all night to the harbor, a shell burst just as they were entering Sumter, and a fellow teenager from Kensington Plantation was killed.

With the exception of the boys who carried messages to the different quarters of the fort day and night, the laborers were arranged in line from the base of the fort to the top of the wall to rebuild those areas shot away during the daylight hours. So began a daily routine. Hour after hour, they passed bags of sand to one another. They were ever vigilant of the Parrott shells and mortars that arrived in five-minute intervals. When the sentinel saw the muzzle flash from Morris Island, he would cry out, scattering the men in all directions. After the shell burst, Stroyer recalled, "The survivors of us, expecting that it would be our turn next, would be picking up, here and there, parts of the severed bodies of our fellow negroes."

After the danger passed, if the men didn't get back in line immediately, the overseer, an Irishman named Mr. DeBurgh, would start screaming at the men to form ranks. If they hesitated, they were clubbed with an iron bar or piece of shell he carried. "Whether the superior officers knew DeBurgh was killing the negroes off as fast as the shells from Fort Wagner or whether they did not know, or did not care," Stroyer wasn't sure. Though he was certain that the chief engineer, John Johnson, was unaware of the treatment of the workmen, he believed Captain. J.C. Mitchell "was not only mean enough to have allowed it, but he was fully heartless himself." He believed that Mitchell, who harbored "a bitter hatred towards the Yankees," was determined to kill the workmen and that if Sumter was abandoned, he would "lock us negroes up in our quarters…and put powder to it and arrange it so that both the negroes and the Yankees should be blown up."

It was a dreary summer of hard, dangerous labor, and Jacob Stroyer wrote after the afternoon thunderstorms "the whole atmosphere wore the pall of death…the mutilated bodies of the negroes, mingled with the black mud and water in the fort yard." The men were locked up during the day in a room called the "Rat-Hole" that Stroyer recalled was "like a sweat box; it was so hot and close that, although we were exposed to death shells when we were turned out to work, we were glad to get into the fresh air." They drew rations of hardtack and salt pork twice a day—in the mornings when they finished their shift and turned in for the day and again between three and four o'clock in the afternoon before they were sent out to work. Since there

An illustration showing the interior view of Fort Sumter in 1864.

were no means of cooking in their quarters, many of the men were killed and wounded as they stood in line to draw their rations.

One evening, the men were brought in to repair the damage sustained that afternoon. When a shell was incoming, they were instructed by the engineers to go to the center of the fort and hug the ground but under no circumstances were they to take shelter in the Lime House on the parade ground. Human nature being what it is, when a sentinel sounded a warning, the men panicked and a dozen crowded into the building. A split second later, a ten-inch mortar crashed into the structure. As new workers rotated in to fill the ranks of the dead, the men began to pick through the wreckage and discovered most of the men were "so mangled that their bodies were not recognizable."

Even the hardened veterans of the Confederacy pitied the plight of the work parties. Sergeant Milton Leverette wrote to his family in the summer of 1864:

> *I have seen a great many wounded and some few killed since being down here. One mortar shell dropped in a crowd of negroes working hitting one outright another died shortly after and wounding ten besides. Poor wretches*

they see a dreadful time of it, are worked very hard and are very much exposed. I feel very sorry for them, some of their masters sending down here without any change of clothes for thirty days at a time. It seems to me I would rather pay a fine or stand a prosecution than send a negro of mine down here especially one I cared for. They are treated entirely too harshly. To be sure the answer would be if the negroes don't do the work the soldier will have to and the alternative is die negro or die soldier consequently the negro gets it, but taking that aside they are treated very harshly by the overseers. [147]

Stroyer was cut over the right eye in the mortar strike and, with the other wounded, was taken to the bombproof in the fort. Looking back on that night, he wrote in 1879:

I shall never forget this first and last visit to the hospital department. To witness the rough handling of the wounded patients, to see them thrown on a table as one would a piece of beef, and to see the doctor use his knife and saw, cutting off a leg, or arm, and sometimes both, with as much indifference as if he were simply cutting up beef, and to hear the doctor say, of almost every other one of these victims, after a leg or an arm was amputated, "Put that fellow in his box," meaning his coffin, was an awful experience.

As Stroyer recovered at Dr. Ragg's hospital in Charleston, the slain were loaded on a boat at Sumter's dock. The next morning, a Parrott shell ripped apart the vessel and the dead sank in their coffins to the bottom of the harbor. Though the bodies were normally taken to the city for burial, Stroyer said that those "so badly cut up by shells, were put into boxes, with pieces of iron in them, and carried a little way from Sumter and thrown overboard." Of the 364 men and boys sent to Sumter that summer, he estimated that forty made it out alive. [148]

There was no reprieve for the survivors, and on June 20, the metal came in hot all day. Trying to escape the noise of the incoming artillery, Captain Mitchell went to a battery on the harbor side of the fort and found no relief. He chatted with his men, telling them that a Parrott shell was preferable to his toothache. He was planning on visiting Charleston the next morning to have the tooth filled.

At twelve o'clock in the afternoon, he was standing on the southwestern angle of the fort inspecting the Union batteries with his field glasses when a sentinel cried, "Lookout!" Just as Mitchell was telling the soldier that he would rather be killed than dodge the Federal shells, he was struck by a mortar *fragment that went through* his thigh and hip "mutilating and mangling it horrible taking out the bone clear." As he lay dying on the surgeon's table, he was fanned by Sergeant Leverette. "Oh my poor mother when she hears of this," Mitchell moaned, "Percy [his adjutant] you must write to my mother, tell her I died like a gentleman at my post fighting gallantly in the same cause as my poor brother Willie only not as gallantly as he as I have screamed more than he." He cried gently and said that he "had hoped to show the garrison how to die, but couldn't help it he was suffering so much pain." Under the effects of the anodyne, he would slip into speaking French though the sentences were disconnected and hard to follow. "He seemed to

Federal mortars aimed at Fort Sumter from batteries on Morris Island.

be speaking in a cheering manner of France, speaking to at one time 'Viva la belle France,'" recalled Leverette. His only regret was that he didn't get promoted to major before being mortally wounded.

Captain Johnson, who would later serve as the rector of St. Phillip's Episcopal Church in Charleston, arrived and asked Mitchell if he could pray for him. He responded by asking for a fatal dose of anodyne to end the pain. The men stayed with the captain, watching the blood soak his clothes and drip on the floor, knowing that every drop shortened his life. After four hours, he died. After some curls were cut off to send to his mother, Mitchell was laid out and dressed in his full captain's uniform, and the body was taken to the fort's office, where a flag was placed over the coffin. Before he died, he asked to be buried at Magnolia Cemetery with no "row" and as "quietly as possible."[149]

At four o'clock that afternoon, twenty-seven-year-old Captain Thomas Abraham Huguenin stationed at Battery Marshall on Sullivan's Island was signaled: "Capt Mitchell is killed, you will take command of Sumter. I need not tell you to hold it." The assignment was a far cry from his student days at The Citadel and his flat in Paris, where he was traveling when news came of South Carolina's secession. He presented his orders to Alfred Rhett at Fort Johnson and informed the colonel that he was anxious to get underway. Rhett said he couldn't prevent his going but advised Huguenin to not cross until dark. The captain was aware of the danger but, under the circumstances, thought it best to get moving. After saying his goodbyes, he started for Sumter in full daylight and reached his post at sunset as the shells boiled the water around him. As he leapt ashore, he saw the coffin containing the body of his predecessor and later admitted, "This was not an inspiring sight, in fact it was a warning of what I might expect my own fate to be."

That evening, Huguenin, accompanied by Captain Johnson, visited every portion of the fort and made notes on the condition of his command. As they approached a scaffold behind the east face, Johnson said, "This is strange. A sentinel should be standing here." They found the man twenty feet below on the parade ground, cut in half by a Parrott shell.

After the inspection, Captain Huguenin determined to secure and rebuild the exterior slope of the gorge. The engineers built a cribwork of heavy timbers, in four squares of ten feet each, from the base of the gorge upward to the top of the lower embrasures. It was at this time that the Federal guns were redirected once again, this time concentrating on the crest of the wall and its eastern angle. Each night, the workmen would rebuild the crest, which was promptly battered away in the next day's bombing.[150]

Death was a near constant, and the garrison came to accept the worst as routine. In one incident, Captain Huguenin and his staff officers were heading to an oyster roast when Lieutenant Therrell with the Thirty-second Georgia came to the office where they were assembled. He was asked to join them for dinner but declined saying he had orders to take charge of a work party. After Huguenin said he would put aside some oysters, Therrell thanked the captain and headed for the parade ground. The officers were still eating when they saw the ambulance corps hauling someone to the hospital that adjoined the mess room to the south. Huguenin went over to

A photograph of Fort Sumter from the sandbar off Morris Island.

see what had happened and discovered that Lieutenant Therrell was dead, along with a number of the black laborers who were working under his direction. It was less than twenty minutes since they had spoken.

The fort's permanent staff officers were daily reminded of the tenuousness of life by the reserve supply of coffins stowed in the same casemate they quartered in. Captain Huguenin recalled that the coffins were used as a sort of table, and one of the officers happened to be sitting near them "and as some people will carelessly do, scribbled his name on one of them." He was unsettled to see the coffin sitting there the next day and urged the quartermaster to use it without regard to its suitability for the occupant. When it was used a couple of days later, the officer was very much relieved, "saying he had been afraid it might be used for himself."

In addition to the Union artillery, the garrison had to contend with the unhealthiness of the post. Their "cot by the sea" was described by Sumter's ordnance sergeant as "a great brick and dirt fort with crowds of rats and fleas." The heat was suffocating. The mosquitoes tormented them day and night. The surgeons saw the effects of yellow fever transmitted by *Aedes aegypti*: jaundiced yellowish faces, high fevers, severe headaches, muscle cramps, dehydration and fatigue, muscular aches, nausea and bloody vomiting. There wasn't enough water or soap to wash either men or clothes, and the place smelled of dirty soldiers and "horrid smelling incendiary shells." And when the men lay down to sleep, they were plagued by parasites. Sergeant Leverette recalled that no matter what time of night, there was someone sitting up in his bed, staring at the wall and scratching and cursing the fleas. After sitting in silence a while, he would go over and shake another soldier and ask him if he was sleeping. Soon everyone was awake and, as Leverette wrote, "having one grand scratching party." Though he wasn't injured in defense of the post, he told his sister that he was scarred from the fleas that fed on him nightly.

Sumter was a tough assignment and the men survived on quinine pills, bacon, loaf bread that tasted like sawdust and hardtack, which one soldier described as "the most indigestible kind of food." The fort did hold a special place in the hearts of Charlestonians, and that afforded certain perks. Leverette was summoned one evening to Captain Huguenin's office, where he expected to be reprimanded for some unknown offense but was instead pointed to a table with several cakes and hot whiskey punch. He made a "vigorous attack" on the sweets but assured his mother in a letter home that he passed on the whiskey. She was pleased with his strength of character, writing to him that alcohol "inflames the blood, and makes a man like a beast in his conduct."

Another evening, a company of the First South Carolina Regiment of Regular Infantry, composed almost entirely of Irishmen, was brought in to repair the day's damages. It was a tough detail, but that evening, the Ladies' Relief Association of Charleston sent over some food. At daybreak, the fatigue parties received rations of whiskey and watermelon. The next day, an officer overheard one of the Irishmen say, "'I say, Pat, how dow you like soldiering in Sumter!" The reply came immediately: "By Jabers! Who would'nt soldier in Sumter with melons and whiskey?" These luxuries were by no means available in other posts in the harbor. As one private reported, "We are seeing hard time we haven't had any meat for five days, dry cracker is all we have to eat, out of sixteen days rashans we have only got meat five times. That is enough to make a man swear I hate to write home about our fair, but it gets wors and wors evry day." The situation was nearly as bad for the Union forces serving in the Charleston Harbor. Lieutenant William T. Sampson serving onboard the USS *Patapsco* wrote that there "is not a prepared dish placed upon the table that does not contain a large proportion of roaches." He estimated that he ate at least twenty a day, though he tried to avoid the larger ones. When he lay down, he wrote to his wife, "Millions travel over me every night, crawling into my nose, ears, eyes, & mouth."[151]

As the garrison settled into a routine, the men found time to play cards and chess, anything to pass the time. The men liked receiving letters, though one soldier asked his family not to mail baskets since the "soldiers steal too freely." Given the fort's namesake, it's fitting that gamecock fighting was popular and the officers often signaled their counterparts at Forts Moultrie and Johnson that they were bringing their birds over for a fight. Captain Huguenin's "most pugnacious" and accomplished gamecock named Dick, after Fighting Dick Anderson with the Army of Northern Virginia, was left behind at Battery Marshall when he assumed command of Fort Sumter. When he was informed by his body servant, Frank, that the young officers of the regiment were fighting his bird at Fort Johnson, he sent a boat to collect him.

In the predawn hours of July 28, the gamecock began to crow on his perch in Huguenin's office. Aiming to have a little fun, the captain tucked the bird under his arm and headed to the parapet at the southeast angle to wake his enemies on Morris Island. He reported that the gamecock "crowed most vigorously," and soon the Union artillerists responded by chucking in a few shells. Captain John Johnson was inspecting the nearby angle of the gorge and was injured when a mortar exploded over the fort. His loss was a severe blow to the garrison and Huguenin assumed engineering duties until the arrival of Lieutenant Edwin J. White two days later.[152]

A photograph showing the interior of Fort Sumter with gabion reinforcements.

As the summer wore on, the spirits of the garrison flagged. Day after day, night after night, the iron poured in, incessant and demoralizing. The situation reached a critical point after Huguenin discovered that members of the Thirty-second Georgia Regulars disobeyed orders and were resting in their quarters rather than waiting in reserve should the fort come under amphibious assault. The lieutenant and several of the men were placed under arrest. The next morning, several Georgian troops appeared in the hallway outside Huguenin's office to retrieve their friends. The captain jerked the ringleader into his office and had him held with a gun to his head with orders to "blow his brains out" if he resisted. The remaining Georgians rushed back to get their weapons, and now Huguenin faced an armed revolt. Expecting "bloody work in that passageway that afternoon," the captain ordered a howitzer loaded with grape and canister and a company brought forward with rifles.

With the garrison locked in an armed standoff, Captain George W. Lamar, the commissary and quartermaster of the fort, appealed to his fellow Georgians to remember their duty and stand down. He also warned the men that "not one man of you who enters that passage will leave it alive." After a pause and some talk among the men, they retired to quarters thinking the matter settled. Huguenin telegraphed headquarters and asked that the Thirty-second be relieved and sent an armed detachment to the western barracks to arrest the Georgians. The men were shackled and placed under armed guard before being sent to the city the following morning. Three

This photograph shows a breach patched with gabions on the north wall of Fort Sumter.

conspirators were executed by firing squad, while the rest were pardoned at the captain's urging.

After the mutiny, Sergeant Milton Leverette's family urged him to resign his post at Fort Sumter and take up blockade running because "there was no honor to be in Sumter now." His mother warned that he needed to flee that "den of gamblers and drunkards," fearing "some judgment [from] the Almighty, will come down on a place where so much wickedness is prevailing." Though he would not abandon his post, he confided in his father that his faith had been tested by the events of the past few months.

While the Confederates were feuding among themselves, J.G Foster decided to break the stalemate of the previous months. The plan was to breach a wall of Fort Sumter using a raft loaded with explosives and towed by a large rowboat. On August 28, after several unsuccessful attempts the previous month, Foster made his final effort to bring down the wall. The newest raft was made of two-inch oak plank and contained 2,800 pounds of powder. The Yankees waited for a dark, moonless night and set off for the north side of Fort Sumter. Private T.F. Haines, on picket duty with the Twelfth New York Infantry, recalled, "This torpedo had a fuse to burn estimated at a certain time of tide while a boat was drifting 40 yards, connected with a sub-marine fuse in a pistol held by Lieut. Abercrombie. Every one [on] that crew knew the Lieutenant would not fire the fuse till we were as near the fort as 40 yards. We had to pull by the fort in plain sight of the Johnnies to get above, when we could get down." Though they were dressed to swim and wearing only shirts, the men were armed with Sharp's rifles, navy revolvers and cutlasses.

As the raft edged closer to Fort Sumter, the Union troops could see the outlines of the Confederate sentries on the parapet oblivious to their approach. "The north side of the fort looked like a large motel, with the ports open and lighted up," recalled Haines. A few dozen yards out, Lieutenant Abercrombie lit the fuse. Within seconds, the Confederates, thinking that the Federals were attempting to storm the fort, were crowded on the walls pouring in fire from above. As the Blue Backs rowed back toward Morris Island, the raft drifted into a corner pile dock and was turned aside by the tide. As the Rebels ran for cover, the raft exploded about thirty feet from where it was designed to go, "blowing the dock as high as could see." Aside from being "liberally splattered with mud," Huguenin reported that the garrison was unharmed.[153]

The situation, already bad, was now to take an ugly, cynical turn. General Foster had six hundred Confederate prisoners of war delivered from the Fort Delaware Prison on August 20. They were placed on starvation rations and

An interior view of Fort Sumter showing ruins, taken by a Confederate photographer in 1864.

housed in a one-and-a-half-acre pen directly between Sumter and Foster's artillery on Morris Island. "Just imagine our position," one Confederate recorded in his journal, "tied hands and feet...without the means of defending ourselves and know not what moment we may be writhing and bleeding under the effects of the bursting of terrible shell." Week after week, the prisoners watched as the Union artillery crashed into the walls of Sumter. When the Confederates responded with their own guns, they prayed the shells didn't fall short.

A photograph of Fort Johnson with Fort Sumter in the distance.

Major General Jones was irate, and on September 7, he wrote to the Confederate military command, "If the department thinks it proper to retaliate by placing Yankee officers in Sumter or other batteries, let the order be given, prompt action should be taken." His plan for parading Union soldiers on the walls of Sumter was ignored as the War Department had more pressing concerns to deal with.[154]

As Jones waited for an answer that would never come, the Federal shelling on Sumter began to taper off, and by mid-September, after sixty-seven days, the bombardment ended due to a lack of ammunition.[155] The garrison survived everything the Feds threw at it, but with General Tecumseh

Fort Sumter after it was abandoned.

Sherman burning his way across Georgia, the coastal defenses were now irrelevant. Everyone knew the war was winding down, and the Confederates were marching slowly backward toward defeat. The South wasn't ready to accept that unhappy fact, but there it was, nonetheless.

8
END GAME

Many of Fort Sumter's garrison grew up on plantations along the South Carolina coast or in the fine-looking houses on the Charleston Battery. Its members were graduates of The Citadel and Harvard. They traveled in Europe. In 1860, they celebrated as their native state declared it was no longer in the American Union. As soldiers and officers of the Confederate army, many spent most of the Civil War practically within sight of their homes, guarding Charleston Harbor until the night of February 17, 1865. It was exactly one year after the *H.L. Hunley* sank the *Housatonic*.[156]

After 212 days of command, Huguenin had the two battle flags that had flown for the sixty-day bombardment lowered and sent to the city. After a new flag was raised, the men formed ranks and boarded two steamers tied off at the sally port. As the men waited, the captain ascended the wrecked parapet one last time and took survey of his post. When he reached the ship at midnight, he was overcome with emotion as he ordered the lines cut. His heart sank as he watched Sumter disappear into the darkness. He wanted to stay and fight, to die in defense of the fort, but the captain had his orders. Two days later, on February 19, 1864, Fort Sumter fell without a fight to the Union.

On April 12, 1864, news reached Charleston that Lee's Army of Northern Virginia had surrendered. By this time, the city was crowded with visitors from the North to celebrate. The next morning, they would hoist the American flag over Fort Sumter on the four-year anniversary of Major Anderson's surrender. Senator Wilson of Massachusetts and General Washburn each addressed the crowd that evening and patriotic tunes were

This photograph shows Charleston after the surrender to Federal forces. The damage was not a result of the war bombing but of the Great Fire of 1861 that began on December 11 and could be seen by Confederate troops fourteen miles away.

played by the 14th Maine and 127th New York Regiment bands. It was a party not to be forgotten.

At an early hour, the note of preparation was sounded, salvos of artillery were fired and every vessel in the harbor made steam toward Fort Sumter. The weather was perfect with clear blue skies and a gentle breeze from the east. With the exception of Sumter, the American flag was seen floating from all the harbor's principal fortifications.

The whole morning was spent in transporting the large numbers of visitors to Sumter, which was entered on the northeast side by a flight of wooden steps, leading to the demolished parapet. The visitors found the fort

A Federal squadron dressed with flags for the anniversary of Major Robert Anderson's surrender in 1861 seen from a parapet of Fort Sumter.

a jumbled mess of debris composed of concrete, brick and sand littered with unexploded artillery shells.

Standing on a platform, overlooking the crowd assembled in the parade ground, with the gunboats and monitors and steamers lying a short distance off, was Reverend Henry Ward Beecher, an abolitionist that spent his pre–Civil War years raising funds to buy rifles, called "Beecher Bibles," for antislavery forces in the territories. There were over two hundred naval officers present, including Admiral Dahlgren and Commodore Rowan. Generals Gillmore, Anderson, Dix, Washburn, Doubleday, Delafield, Grover, Hatch, Saxton and Molineux were there, along with Adjunct General Townsend and Colonel Gurney, commanders of the post.

Notable citizens present were Senator Wilson, William Lloyd Garrison, Samuel Harper and ex-governor Clifford of Massachusetts; Lieutenant

Governor Anderson of Ohio; Justice Swaine of the Supreme Court of the United States; Judges Strong and Thompson and Congressman Kelly of Pennsylvania; George Thompson of England; and General Anderson's wife and children. There were also large detachments of white and African American troops, including the Fifty-fourth Massachusetts, whose fallen comrades lay rotting two miles south in the shallow, sandy soils of Morris Island. All total, it is estimated that at least three thousand people were present, though there wasn't a Southerner in sight to watch this sad, stupid spectacle.

The ceremony started with the singing of "Victory at Last," followed by the reading of scripture by Chaplain Harris, who made the prayer at the raising of the flag when Major Anderson moved his command from Fort Moultrie to Sumter. The old flag was brought forward to roaring applause, and Anderson stepped forward and told the audience "I thank God I have lived to see this day, to be here to perform this perhaps the last act of duty to my country in this life. My heart is filled with gratitude to Almighty God for the signal blessings which he has given us—blessings beyond number. May all the world proclaim glory to God in the highest, on earth peace and good will toward men."

As soon as he finished his remarks, the flag was raised and when it caught a breeze, the crowd went wild. One witness recalled, "It was an inspiring moment, grand and sublime, never to be experienced again." The flag was saluted with one hundred guns from Sumter and with a "national salute" from Fort Moultrie and Battery Bee on Sullivan's Island, Fort Putnam on Morris Island and Fort Johnson on James Island. As the band died down, the crowd broke into the "Star-Spangled Banner."

Next up was Reverend Beecher, the chief orator of the day. He told the multitude gathered on the parade ground:

> *These shattered heaps of shapeless stones are all that is left of Fort Sumter. Desolation broods in yonder sad city. Solemn retribution hath avenged our dishonored banner. You have come back with honor who departed hence four years ago, leaving the air sultry with fanaticism. The surging crowds that rolled up their frenzied shouts as the flag came down are dead, or scattered, or silent, and their habitations are desolate. Ruin sits in the cradle of treason, rebellion has perished, but there flies the same flag that was insulted.*

He offered precious few words of reconciliation or healing, telling the spectators, "Vengeance is mine, I will repay, saith the Lord." Before offering congratulations and good health to President Lincoln, he reminded the defeated that "this flag commands not supplicates. There may be pardon,

Flag-raising ceremony, with Brevet Major General Robert Anderson and Henry Ward Beecher present along with three thousand others from the North to celebrate the taking of Fort Sumter.

but no concession. There may be amnesty and oblivion, but no honied [*sic*] compromises. The nation to-day has peace for the peaceful, and war for the turbulent. The only condition of submission is to submit." The audience broke into thunderous applause.[157]

The next day, on the evening of April 14, 1865, while attending a performance of the comedy *Our American Cousin* at Ford's Theatre, Abraham Lincoln was shot by John Wilkes Booth. It was four years to the day after Anderson saluted his flag and handed Fort Sumter to the Confederates. Nine hours later, at 7:22 a.m. on April 15, the president was dead.

NOTES

Chapter 1

1. Gleig, *History*.
2. *New York Times*, June 2, 1814.
3. U.S. Government, General Records, *Treaty of Ghent*.
4. Clay, *Life and Speeches*, 231–32.
5. Madison, "Seventh State of Nation."
6. Lewis, *Seacoast Fortifications*, 37, 87–9.
7. Pemberton, *Fort Sumter*. The decision to name the installation after General Thomas Sumter did not take place until after his death in 1832.
8. Lieutenant Henry Brewerton, Corp of Engineers, to Ralph Berkley, September 15, 1829; Henry Brewerton to Brigadier General Charles Gratiot, chief engineer with Corp of Engineers, July 1, 1830. Letters are located in the Fort Sumter Vertical File. The development of the rock mole is depicted in a plat found in drawer 66, sheet 2 at Fort Moultrie.
9. U.S. Congress, House Documents, 3–4.
10. Pickett, *History of Alabama*, 606–08.
11. Message of Governor Hayne, 165–71.
12. *Charleston Mercury*, January 10, 1838.
13. Fraser, *Charleston!*, 206.
14. Edgar, *South Carolina*, 326–27.
15. "Letters from Thomas Jefferson," 212.
16. Fraser, *Charleston!*, 213.

17. *Addresses and Messages.*
18. Bassett, *Life of Andrew Jackson*, 34.
19. Quoted in Bouche, *Nullification Controversy*, 284.
20. Meacham, *American Lion*, 240.
21. Latner, "Nullification Crisis," 19–38; Meacham, *American Lion*, 483.
22. Edgar, *South Carolina*, 336.
23. "Construction of Fort Sumter," *American State Papers*, 463–72.
24. Calhoun, *Speeches of John C. Calhoun*, 82, 230–33; Calhoun, *Papers of John C. Calhoun*, 12:181; 13:81–82, 86, 186, 480, 482; 14:103; Robert Remini, *Henry Clay*, 1.

CHAPTER 2

25. Coleman and Custer, "Cultural Resources Study," 19; Clary, *Fortress America*, 27–39.
26. General Totten to A.H. Bowman, January 11, 1841, transcribed copy located in the Fort Sumter Vertical File; Captain A.G. Bowman to General Totten, June 15, 1851, transcribed letter located in the Fort Sumter Vertical File.
27. A list of brickyards under contract to Fort Sumter was compiled by its staff and provided to me by park historian Rick Hatcher; Funk, *Three Rivers*, 192–93.
28. Barnes, *Fort Sumter*, 9; Lieutenant Colonel R.E. DeRussy, commander of Corp of Engineers, to S. Thayer, March 14, 1851. The letter is included in the correspondence of the U.S. Army Corps of Engineers officers assigned to work on the fortifications in Charleston Harbor from August 12, 1854, to April 2, 1861. The Fort Sumter "Letter Book" is in the collections of the Charleston Museum.
29. DeRussy to Thayer, March 14, 1851.
30. Lewis, *Seacoast Fortifications*, 60.
31. Lieutenant Colonel J. Erving to Lieutenant J.D. Kurts, May 13, 1851, transcribed copy located in the Fort Sumter Vertical File.
32. Ibid.; Stryker, *Stryker's American Register*, 567.
33. Proceedings of the meeting of delegates from the Southern Rights Associations of South Carolina.
34. Edgar, *South Carolina*, 344.
35. Lieutenant Kurtz to General Totten, May 15, 1851, transcribed copy located in the Fort Sumter Vertical File.

36. Edgar, *South Carolina*, 345.

37. Davis. *Rhett*, 64.

38. Edgar, *South Carolina*, 345–47.

39. Obadele-Starks, *Freebooters*, 161.

40. *Charleston Courier*, September 3, 1858; *Columbia Guardian*, September 4, 1858.

41. Sinha, *Counterrevolution*, 153–54, 156.

42. Herb Frazier, "In Search of Emancipation: Illegal Slave Trade and Return to Africa," *Charleston Mercury*, July 26, 2011; John Grimball family papers; Charles Thomson Haskell family papers.

43. Daniel H. Hamilton Case Records; *New York Times*, November 27, 1858; quoted in *Cleveland Herald*, July 29, 1859.

44. Quotes found in the *Cleveland Plain Dealer*, May 23, 1859, and *Ohio State Journal*, May 17, 1859.

CHAPTER 3

45. Crawford, *History*, 29.

46. Official Report of Major F.J. Porter, War Department, November 11, 1860, found in Crawford, *History*, 59; Fraser, *Charleston!*, 245.

47. Johnson and Buel, *Battles and Leaders*, 43.

48. Correspondence between Governor William Henry Gist and Assistant Secretary William Henry Trescott.

49. J.G. Foster to Colonel R.E. DeRussy, November 24, 1860, Letter Book. For a detailed description of the events in Charleston Harbor immediately before the Civil War, see Crawford, *Genesis*, 296–304 and U.S. War Department, *War of the Rebellion*, 1:74.

50. Johnson and Buel, *Battles and Leaders*, 43.

51. Major Robert Anderson to Adjutant General Cooper, November 28, 1860, in U.S. War Department, *War of the Rebellion*, 1:79, 98; Foster to DeRussy, November 30, 1860, Fort Sumter "Letter Book"; Anderson to Cooper, November 28, 1860; Johnson and Buel, *Battles and Leaders*, 1, 42.

52. Johnson and Buel, *Battles and Leaders*, 42; *New York Times*, April 8, 1861.

53. U.S. War Department, *War of the Rebellion*, 1:95–96.

54. Crawford, *Genesis*, 70, 77–78.

55. Crawford, *Genesis*, 70–78.

56. Pryor, *My Day*, 153–54; Kelly, *Best Little Stories*, 8.

57. U.S. War Department, *War of the Rebellion*, 1:89.

58. Doubleday, *Reminiscences*, 57, 62–66; Johnson and Buel, *Battles and Leaders*, 45.

NOTES TO PAGES 49−61

59. Fant, "Castle Pinckney"; Higgins, "History."
60. Johnson and Buel, *Battles and Leaders*, 53; U.S. War Department, *War of the Rebellion*, 19; Davis, *Rhett*, 437; Fraser, *Charleston!*, 246−47.
61. "Capt. Mcgowan's Report; Steamship Star of the West," *New York Times*, January 14, 1861; *Harper's Weekly*, January 26, 1861; Doubleday, *Reminiscences*, 102.
62. War Department to Major Robert Anderson, February 23, 1861, found in Andrews, *History*.
63. U.S. War Department, *War of the Rebellion*, 1:189, 197, 202; Crawford, *Genesis*, 269−70.
64. Fraser, *Charleston!*, 249; *Charleston Mercury*, March 5, 1861; see telegrams of L.P. Walker, Pickens and others in Pickens-Bonham Papers; Lincoln, Farewell Address; Lincoln, First Inaugural Address; Sandburg, *Abraham Lincoln*, 188; Perret, *Lincoln's War*, 3.
65. *New York Times*, "The Choice Is Charybdis," March 23−29, 1861.
66. Williams, *P.G.T. Beauregard*, 34−50.
67. *New York Times*, "Important Correspondence Preceding The Bombardment," April 13, 1861; Fraser, *Charleston!*, 248−49; Chesnut, *Original Civil War Diaries*, 41−46.
68. *New York Times*, April 5, 1861, 30−31.
69. Lamon, *Recollections*, 71; Klingaman, *Abraham Lincoln*, 30; Foote, *Fort Sumter*, 48; Perret, *Lincoln's War*, 20.
70. U.S. War Department, *War of the Rebellion*, 1:236−40. If the president had any doubts how the expedition would be received, they were answered on April 3 when batteries on Morris Island opened up on the merchant ship *Rhoda H. Shannon* out of Boston that mistakenly believed it was in Savannah.
71. Sandburg, *Abraham Lincoln*, 224; Robert Toombs to Jefferson Davis, in "Clarion Calls of Defiance," *New York Times*, April 3−9, 1861.
72. Foote, *Fort Sumter*, 49; Chesnut, *Original Civil War Diaries*, 141−46; *New York Times*, April 14, 1861.
73. Doubleday, *Reminiscences*, 39; Fraser, *Charleston!*, 250; Johnson and Buel, *Battles and Leaders*, 71−75, 79−80; *New York Times*, April 18, 1865; *New York Times*, April 19, 1861; Spicer, *Flag Replaced on Sumter*, 8; Williams, "From Sumter to the Wilderness," 1−11, 93−104.

CHAPTER 4

74. Johnson, *Defense of Charleston Harbor*, 18; "Roswell Sabin Ripley," 225–42; U.S. War Department, *War of the Rebellion*, 35:632–34.

75. *Charleston Mercury*, July 8, 1861.

76. Johnson, *Defense of Charleston Harbor*, 39; Fraser, *Charleston!*, 257; *Charleston Mercury*, December 1, 1862; Fraser, *Charleston!*, 252.

77. *Charleston Mercury*, November 28, 1861.

78. Ibid., June 30, 1863; Burton, *Siege of Charleston*, 99; *Life, Letters and Speeches*, 494.

79. "Capture of Charleston—First Instructions."

80. *New York Times*, "IRON-CLADS; The Navy Department and Admiral Dupont. Dupont's Opinion of Our Armored Vessels. THE LAST ATTACK ON CHARLESTON. An Important and Interesting Official Report," April 16, 1864; Burton, *Siege of Charleston*, 135; Weddle, "'Fall of Satan's Kingdom,'" 411–39.

81. Thompson and Wainwright, *Confidential Correspondence*, 160 (Samuel F. Du Pont to Gustavus V. Fox, October 8, 1862); Welles, *Diary*, 158; U.S. War Department, *War of the Rebellion*, 13:376 (Gideon Welles to John Dahlgren, October 8, 1862).

82. Fehrenbacher and Fehrenbacher, *Recollected Words* , 380; Welles, *Diary*, 259, 265 (April 2, 1863); Burlingame, *Lincoln Observed*, 213.

83. *New York Times*, November 13, 1889; Hunter and Chamberlin, *Sketches*, 111–12.

84. Johnson, *Defense of Charleston Harbor*, 109, 37–39; Editors of Time-Life Books, *Voices of the Civil War*, 50.

85. *Cornhill Magazine*, 102; Johnson, *Defense of Charleston Harbor*, 50.

86. Johnson, *Defense of Charleston Harbor*, 49; *Charleston Mercury*, April 11, 1863.

87. U.S. War Department, *War of the Rebellion*, 14:10–12.

88. Report of Commander John Downes.

89. *Military Essays and Recollections*, 195–96; Editors of Time-Life Books, *Voices of the Civil War*, 55.

90. *New York Times*, "The Bombardment of Sumter. Letters from on Board the Iron-Clads. The Keokuk. the Nantucket. the Nahant," April 17, 1863.

91. U.S. War Department, *War of the Rebellion*, 1:437.

92. A. Lincoln Telegram to Admiral S.F. Du Pont, Executive Mansion, Washington, April 13, 1863; Basler, *Collected Works*, 16.

93. A. Lincoln to General D. Hunter and Admiral S.F. Du Pont, Executive Mansion, Washington, April 14, 1863; Basler, *Collected Works*, 16.

94. Welles, *Diary*, 273 (April 15, 1863).
95. *New York Times*, June 11, 1863; Whitelaw, *History of Ohio*; *New York Times*, "The Relations of Admiral Dahlgren and Gen. Gillmore—What Admiral Dahlgren Hopes to Accomplish and What is Expected of Him," October 22, 1863.
96. Johnson, *Defense of Charleston Harbor*, 57–58, 78–79, 108–09, 111.
97. Roman, *Military Operations*, 111, 118; Denison, *Shot and Shell*, 162; Ripley, "Correspondence," 5.
98. Gilchrist, *Confederate Defence*, 7; Roman, *Military Operations*, 114.
99. Copp, *Reminiscences*, 225.
100. Ibid., 226–27.
101. Olmstead, "Reminiscences," 8.
102. Editors of Time-Life Books, *Voices of the Civil War*, 82; also see Gillmore, *Engineer and Artillery Operations* and Gilchrist, *Confederate Defence*.
103. Johnson, *Defense of Charleston Harbor*, 98–101; Copp, *Reminiscences*, 204–06.
104. Addresses Delivered Before Confederate Survivors Association, 10. For further reading on the operations against Morris Island and Battery Wagner see Wise, *Gate of Hell*; Emilio, *Brave Black Regiment*; Gillmore, *Engineer and Artillery Operations*.
105. Hunter and Chamberlin, *Sketches*, 326; Johnson, *Defense of Charleston Harbor*, 100–02; see also Roman, *Military Operations*; U.S. War Department, *War of the Rebellion*, 28; Denison, *Shot and Shell*; Gilchrist, *Confederate Defence*; Gillmore, *Engineer and Artillery Operations*; Johnson, *Defense of Charleston Harbor*; Gillmore, *Engineer and Artillery Operations*; Roman, *Military Operations*.
106. Gillmore, *Engineer and Artillery Operations*.
107. Editors of Time-Life Books, *Voices of the Civil War*, 91–93.
108. Ibid., 92–93.
109. Hunter and Chamberlin, *Sketches*, 329.
110. Editors of Time-Life Books, *Voices of the Civil War*, 105–09.
111. Lewis Henry Douglass (1840–1908) to Helen Amelia Loguen, July 20, 1863, Carter G. Woodson Papers, Manuscript Division, Library of Congress Transcription.
112. See Gillmore, 1865; Gilchrist, *Confederate Defence*, 28; U.S. War Department, *War of the Rebellion*, 28.
113. Alexander, "Four Frustrating Years."

CHAPTER 5

114. *Military Essays and Recollections,* 196.

115. Foote, *Fort Sumter,* 184; Editors of Time-Life Books, *Voices of the Civil War,* 117; See *The War of the Rebellion,* Volume 14:437–46; Johnson, *Defense of Charleston Harbor,* 116-121; Burton, *Seige of Charleston,* 185.

116. C.L. Burckmyer correspondence; editors of Time-Life Books, *Voices of the Civil War,* 19, 21; Burton, 186; Roman, *Military Operations,* 147; Fraser, *Charleston!,* 265; William S. Stryker, "The Swamp Angel," in Johnson and Buel, *Battles and Leaders,* 73–74.

117. Burton, *Siege of Charleston,* 187; *New York Herald,* August 26, 1863.

118. Roman, *Military Operations,* 147; *Charleston Mercury,* September 2, 1863; editors of Time-Life Books, *Voices of the Civil War,* 117, 128.

119. Editors of Time-Life Books, *Voices of the Civil War,* 130, 132; *Military Essays and Recollections,* 221.

120. Gillmore, *Engineer and Artillery Operations*; Gilchrist, *Confederate Defence*; Johnson, *Defense of Charleston Harbor*; U.S. War Department, *War of the Rebellion,* 28; Copp, *Reminiscences,* 273–74.

121. Johnson, *Defense of Charleston Harbor,* 156; Alexander, "Four Frustrating Years"; editors of Time-Life Books, *Voices of the Civil War,* 136–37.

122. *New York Herald,* "The Siege of Charleston. The Assault. To the Editor of the Herald," October 19, 1863.

123. Letters of Stephen Elliott; *Charleston Mercury,* November 3, 1863.

CHAPTER 6

124. *New York Herald,* "Charleston. The Third Bombardment of Sumter. Commencement and Progress of the Third Bombardment," November 8, 1863.

125. *Charleston Mercury,* November 11, 1863.

126. *New York Herald,* "Charleston. The Third Bombardment of Sumter. Commencement and Progress of the Third Bombardment," November 8, 1863; *Charleston Mercury,* November 11, 1863.

127. Letters of Stephen Elliott.

128. Quoted in Fraser, *Charleston!,* 264.

129. *New Bedford Mercury,* November 17, 1863; *New York Times,* November 9, 1863.

130. *New Bedford Mercury,* November 17, 1863.

131. Johnson, *Defense of Charleston Harbor,* 177.

132. Ibid., 182

133. Johnson, *Defense of Charleston Harbor*, 182; editors of Time-Life Books, *Voices of the Civil War*, 126. The operation was supervised by Lieutenant W. Gourdin Young of the Corp of Engineers working from his office in Charleston. He was later replaced by F.M. Hall, who served as assistant engineer at the fort.

134. *New Bedford Mercury*, December 4, 1863.

135. Johnson, *Defense of Charleston Harbor*, 191.

136. Letters of Stephen Elliott.

137. Johnson, *Defense of Charleston Harbor*, 191.

138. Ibid., 193.

139. Ibid.

140. Letters of Stephen Elliott.

141. *New Bedford Mercury*, January 7, 1864.

142. *News and Courier*, September 7, 1963; Johnson, *Defense of Charleston Harbor*, 196.

143. Johnson, *Defense of Charleston Harbor*, 197.

144. Ibid., 202.

145. Joseph L. Galloway, "Purloined Poison Letters: Fake or Real, They Raised Hell," *US News*, June 7, 2000; *New Bedford Mercury*, June 14, 1864.

CHAPTER 7

146. Johnson, *Defense of Charleston Harbor*, 225.

147. Taylor, Matthews and Power, *Leverett Letters*, 310–11, 345–46; Stroyer, *My Life*, 38–46.

148. Cauthen, *South Carolina*, 178–87; Stroyer, *My Life*, 38–46. Stroyer's observations run contrary to causality lists. In September 1864, the garrison included 195 officers and soldiers and 120 slaves. Of the dozen men killed during the third major bombardment of Sumter, eleven were African American laborers.

149. Taylor, Matthews and Power, *Leverett Letters*, 345–46.

150. Huguenin, *Journal*; Johnson, *Defense of Charleston Harbor*, 228.

151. Taylor, Matthews and Power, *Leverett Letters*, 309, 330; Huguenin, *Journal*; Editors of Time-Life Books, *Voices of the Civil War*, 151.

152. Johnson, *Defense of Charleston Harbor*, 231; Taylor, Matthews and Power, *Leverett Letters*, 310; Huguenin, *Journal*.

153. Taylor, Matthews and Power, *Leverett Letters*, 351, 364, 369, 370; Huguenin, *Journal*; editors of Time-Life Books, *Voices of the Civil War*, 152–53.
154. Cunningham, "Prisoners Under Fire," 28.
155. Johnson, *Defense of Charleston Harbor*, 236–37.

CHAPTER 8

156. Sherman's troops arrived on the outskirts of Columbia, South Carolina, the day before the evacuation of Fort Sumter.
157. The Living Age, May 6, 1865: 193–195, 202; *New York Times*, "Fort Sumter; Restoration of the Stars and Stripes. Solemn and Impressive Ceremonies. Gen. Anderson Hoists the Old Sumter Flag Over the Ruins of the Fort. It Is Saluted By Hundreds Of Guns. Affecting Speech by General Anderson. Eloquent and Impressive Address by Rev. H.W. Beecher. A voice from the North to the South," April 18, 1865.

BIBLIOGRAPHY

PRIMARY

The Addresses and Messages of the Presidents of the United States, Together with the Declaration of Independence and the Constitution of the United States. New York: McClean and Taylor, 1839.

Addresses Delivered Before the Confederate Survivors' Association in Augusta, Georgia. Augusta, GA: Jowitt & Shaver, Printers, 1892.

Basler, Roy P., ed. *Collected Works of Abraham Lincoln.* Vol. 6. New Brunswick, NJ: Rutgers University Press, 1953.

Burlingame, Michael, ed. *Lincoln Observed: Civil War Dispatches of Noah Brooks.* Baltimore, MD: Johns Hopkins University Press, 1998.

Calhoun, John Caldwell. *The Papers of John C. Calhoun.* Edited by Clyde Wilson. Columbia: University of South Carolina Press, 1979.

————. *The Speeches of John C. Calhoun: Delivered in the Congress of the United States from 1811 to Present.* New York: Harper & Brothers.

"The Capture of Charleston—First Instructions." [Confidential.] Navy Department, May 13, 1862. *Report of the Secretary of the Navy in Relation to Armored Vessels.* Washington, D.C.: United States Printing Office, 1864.

Chesnut, Mary Boykin. *The Original Civil War Diaries of Mary Boykin Chesnut.* Edited by Mary Boykin Miller, C. Vann Woodward and Elisabeth Muhlenfeld. New York: Oxford University Press, 1985.

Clay, Henry. *The Life and Speeches of the Hon. Henry Clay.* Vol. 1. Edited by Daniel Mallory. Gale: Sabin Americana, 1857.

"The Construction of Fort Sumter, Charleston Harbor, South Carolina." *American State Papers: Documents Legislative and Executive of the Congress of the United States, Military Affairs.* Vol. 5. 23rd Cong., 2d sess., no. 591, 463–72.

Copp, Elbridge J. *Reminiscences of the War of the Rebellion, 1861–1865.* Nashua, NH: Telegraph Publishing Company, 1911.

Correspondence between Governor William Henry Gist and Assistant Secretary William Henry Trescott. Located at the South Caroliniana Library, University of South Carolina.

Denison, Fredrick. *Shot and Shell: The Third Rhode Island Heavy Artillery Regiment in the Rebellion, 1861–1865, Providence, R.I.; Third Rhode Island Artillery Veterans Association, 1879.* Providence, RI: J.A. and R.A. Reid, 1879.

Doubleday, Abner, *Reminiscences of Forts Sumter and Moultrie in 1860–'61.* Spartanburg, SC: Reprint Co., 1976.

Editors of Time-Life Books. *Voices of the Civil War: Charleston.* Alexandria, VA: Time-Life Books, 1997.

Emilio, L.F. *A Brave Black Regiment: History of the Fifty-Fourth Regiment of Massachusetts Volunteer Infantry 1863–1865.* 3rd edition. Salem, NH: Ayer Company Publishers, Inc., 1894.

Fehrenbacher, Don E., and Virginia E. Fehrenbacher, ed. *Recollected Words of Abraham Lincoln.* Standford, CA: Stanford University Press, 1996.

Fort Sumter "Letter Book." Collections of the Charleston Museum.

Gillmore, Quincy A. *Engineer and Artillery Operations against the Defences of Charleston Harbor in 1863; Comprising the Descent upon Morris Island, the Demolition of Fort Sumter, the Reduction of Forts Wagner and Gregg. With Observations on Heavy Ordnance, Fortifications, Etc. With the Official Reports of Chief of Artillery, Assistant Engineers, Etc. Illustrated by Seventy-Six Plates and Engraved Views.* New York, D. Van Nostrand, 1865.

Gleig, George Robert. *A History of the Campaigns of the British at Washington and New Orleans.* 1826. Reprinted in Henry Steele Commager and Allan Nevins. *The Heritage of America.* Boston, MA: Little, Brown, 1939.

Huguenin, Thomas Abram. *The Journal of Thomas Abram Huguenin.* Clearwater, SC: Eastern Digital Resources, 2003. Located at Fort Moultrie.

Hunter, Robert, and William Henry Chamberlin, eds. *Sketches of War History, 1861–1865: Papers Read before the Ohio Commandery of the Military Order of the Loyal Legion of the United States, 1883–1888.* Vol. 2. Cincinnati, OH: R. Clarke & Company, 1888.

Johnson, John. *The Defense of Charleston Harbor, Including Fort Sumter and the Adjacent Island: 1863–1865.* New York: Books for Libraries Press, 1970. Reprint.

Johnson, Robert Underwood, and Clarence Clough Buel, eds. *Battles and Leaders of the Civil War: Being for the Most Part Contributions by Union and Confederate Officers.* Vol. 1. New York: Century Co., 1887–88.

Lamon, Ward Hill. *Recollections of Abraham Lincoln, 1847–1865.* Chicago: A.C. McClurg and Company, 1895.

Letter from the Secretary of War transmitting the suspension of work at Fort Sumter in the harbor of Charleston, January 7, 1835. Records of the U.S. Congress. Record Group 11. National Archives.

"Letters from Thomas Jefferson to Judge William Johnson." *South Carolina Historical and Genealogical Magazine* 1 (January 1900).

Life, Letters and Speeches of James Louis Petigru: The Union Man of South Carolina. Washington, D.C.: W.H. Lowdermilk, 1920.

Lincoln, Abraham. Farewell address at Springfield, Illinois, 1861.

———. First Inaugural Address. Monday, March 4, 1861.

Madison, James. "Seventh State of Nation, Washington, DC." December 5, 1815. Edited by George Welling. The American Revolution, an HTML project.

Message of Governor Hayne to the Legislature of South Carolina. Reproduced in full in the *Journal of Political Economy* 1.

Military Essays and Recollections: Papers Read before the Commandery of the State of Illinois, Military Order of the Loyal Legion of the United States. Vols. 1–4. Chicago: A.C. McClurg and Company, 1891–1907.

Obadele-Starks, Ernest. *Freebooters and Smugglers: The Foreign Slave Trade in the United States after 1808.* Little Rock: University of Arkansas Press, 2007.

Olmstead, Colonel Charles H. "Reminiscences of Service with the First Volunteer Regiment of Georgia, Charleston Harbor, in 1863." An address delivered before the Georgia Historical Society, March 3, 1879. Savannah, GA: J.H. Estill, 1879.

Papers Read Before the Ohio Commandery, 1886–1888. Vol. 2. Cincinnati, OH: Robert Clark and Company, 1888.

Pickett, Albert James. *History of Alabama, and Incidentally of Georgia and Mississippi, from the Earliest Period.* Vol. 1. Charleston, SC: Walker and James, 1851.

Plat found in drawer 66, sheet 2 at Fort Moultrie.

Porter, John B. "On the Climate and Salubrity of Fort Moultrie and Sullivan's Island, Charleston Harbour, S.C., with Incidental Remarks on the Yellow Fever of the City of Charleston." *American Journal of the Medical Sciences* 28, no. 55 (July 1854): 21–75.

Proceedings of the meeting of delegates from the Southern Rights Associations of South Carolina. Held at Charleston, May 1851. Southern rights documents. Cooperation meeting held in Charleston, SC, July 29, 1851. Library of Congress.

Pryor, Sara Agnes Rice. *My Day: Reminiscences of a Long Life 1830–1912.* New York: Macmillan Company, 1909.

Report of Commander John Downes, commanding U.S. ironclad *Nahant.* Annual Reports of the Navy Department. Report of the Secretary of the Navy, 1863.

Ripley, R.S. "Correspondence Relating to Fortification of Morris Island and Operations of Engineers, Charleston, S.C., 1863." New York: John J. Caulon, 1878.

Spicer, William Arnold. *The Flag Replaced on Sumter: A Personal Narrative.* Lenox: Harpress Publishing, 2012.

Stroyer, Jacob. *My Life in the South.* Salem, MA: Salem Observer Book and Job Print, 1885.

Taylor, Frances Wallace, Catherine Taylor Matthews and J. Tracy Power, eds. *The Leverett Letters: Correspondence of a South Carolina Family, 1851–1868.* Columbia: University of South Carolina Press, 2000.

Thompson, Robert Means, and Richard Wainwright, eds. *Confidential Correspondence of Gustavus Vasa Fox: Assistant Secretary of the Navy.* Vol. 1. New York: Printed for the Naval History Society by the De Vinne Press, 1918–19.

U.S. Congress. House Documents, otherwise published as Executive Documents. 13th Cong., 2d sess., 1878.

U.S. Government. *Treaty of Ghent, 1814: International Treaties and Related Records, 1778–1974.* General Records of the U.S. Congress. Record Group 11. National Archives.

U.S. War Department. *The War of the Rebellion: A Compilation of the Official Records of the Union and Confederate Armies.* 129 vols. Washington, D.C.: Government Printing Office, 1881–1901.

Welles, Gideon. *Diary of Gideon Welles.* Vol. 1. Boston and New York: Houghton Mifflin Company, 1911.

Whitelaw, Reid. *The History of Ohio during the War and the Lives of Her Generals.* Vol. 1 in *Ohio in the War: Her Statesmen, Generals and Soldiers.* Cincinnati, OH: Robert Clarke Company, 1895; reprint, Google e-book.

Williams, Frank B., Jr., ed. "From Sumter to the Wilderness, Letters of Sergeant James Butler Suddeth, Co. E, 7th Regiment S.C.V." *South Carolina Historical Magazine* 63 (1962).

SECONDARY

Alexander, Joseph H. "Four Frustrating Years, Part I." *Leatherneck Magazine* (November 2007).

Andrews, E. Benjamin. *History of the United States*. Vol. 3. Charleston, SC: Nabu Press, 1902; reprint, 2010.

Barnes, Frank. *Fort Sumter: December 26, 1860 and April 12, 1861*. Charleston, SC: National Park Service, 1949.

Bassett, John Spencer. *The Life of Andrew Jackson*. 2 vols. Garden City, NY: Doubleday, Page & Company, 1909.

Bouche, Chauncey Samuel. *The Nullification Controversy in South Carolina*. Chicago: University of Chicago Press, 1916.

Burton, Milby F. *Siege of Charleston, 1861–1865*. Columbia: University of South Carolina Press, 1970.

Cauthen, Charles Edward. *South Carolina Goes to War, 1860–1865*. Chapel Hill: University of North Carolina Press, 1950.

Clary, David. *Fortress America: The Corps of Engineers, Hampton Roads, and the United States Coastal Defense*. Charlottesville: University Press of Virginia, 1990.

Coleman, Wade Catts Ellis and Jay F. Custer. "A Cultural Resources Study and Management Plan for Fort Delaware State Park." Monograph 1. University of Delaware Department of Anthropology, 1983.

Crawford, Samuel Wylie. *The Genesis of the Civil War; or, The Story of Sumter*. New York: Charles E. Webster and Company, 1896.

———. *The History of the Fall of Fort Sumter: Being an Inside History of the Affairs in South Carolina and Washington, 1860–1, and the Conditions and Events in the South which Brought on the Rebellion; the Genesis of the Civil War*. New York: Francis P. Harper, 1896.

Cunningham, Tim. "Prisoners Under Fire." *America's Civil War* 15, no. 6 (January 2003).

Davis, William C. *Rhett: The Turbulent Life and Times of a Fire-Eater*. Columbia: University of South Carolina Press, 2002.

Edgar, Walter B. *South Carolina: A History*. Columbia: University of South Carolina Press, 1998.

Fant, Mrs. James W. "Castle Pinckney." National Register of Historic Places Nomination and Inventory, May 16, 1970.

Foote, Shelby. *Fort Sumter to Perryville*. Vol. 1, *The Civil War: A Narrative*. New York: Random House, 1958.

Fraser, Walter J. *Charleston! Charleston!: The History of a Southern City*. Columbia: University of South Carolina Press, 1991.

Funk, James. *Three Rivers Form an Ocean:…Vignettes of Life in Charleston.* Bloomington, IN: 1ˢᵗ Books Library, 2003.

Gilchrist, Robert C. *The Confederate Defence of Morris Island Charleston Harbor, by the Troops of South Carolina, Georgia, and North Carolina in the Late War Between the States.* Charleston, SC: News and Courier Book Presses, 1884.

Higgins, Michael P. "History of Castle Pinckney." South Carolina State Ports Authority, July 17, 1992.

Kelly, C. Brian. *Best Little Stories from the Civil War: More Than 100 True Stories.* Nashville, TN: Cumberland House, 2010.

Klingaman, William K. *Abraham Lincoln and the Road to Emancipation, 1861–1865.* New York: Viking, 2001.

Latner, Richard B. "The Nullification Crisis and Republican Subversion." *Journal of Southern History* 44, no.1 (1977).

Lewis, Emmanuel Raymond. *Seacoast Fortifications of the United States: An Introductory History.* Annapolis, MD: Leeward Publications, 1979.

Meacham, Jon. *American Lion: Andrew Jackson in the White House.* New York: Random House, 2008.

Pemberton, Heath L., Jr. *Fort Sumter: Chronological Construction History with Architectural Detail.* Charleston, SC: National Park Service, 1959.

Perret, Geoffrey. *Lincoln's War: The Untold Story of America's Greatest President as Commander in Chief.* New York: Random House, 2004.

Remini, Robert. *Henry Clay: Statesman for the Union.* New York: W.W. Norton & Co, 1991.

Roman, Alfred. *The Military Operations of General Beauregard In the War Between the States 1861 to 1865 Including a Brief Personal Sketch and a Narrative of His Service in the War with Mexico, 1846–8.* New York: Harper and Brothers, Franklin Square, 1884.

"Roswell Sabin Ripley: 'Charleston's Gallant Defender.'" *South Carolina Historical Magazine* 3: 225–42.

Sandburg, Carl. *Abraham Lincoln: The Prairie Years.* New York: Dell Publishing Co., Inc. 1926.

Sinha, Manisha. *The Counterrevolution of Slavery: Politics and Ideology in Antebellum South Carolina.* Chapel Hill: University of North Carolina Press, 2000.

Stryker, James. *Stryker's American Register and Magazine.* Vol. 6. New York: W.M. Morrison, 1853.

Weddle, Kevin J. "'The Fall of Satan's Kingdom': Civil-Military Relations and the Union Navy's Attack on Charleston, April 1863." *Journal of Military History* 75, no. 2 (April 2011).

Williams, Harry T. *P.G.T. Beauregard, Napoleon in Gray*. Chaps. 3, 4, 11 and 12. Louisiana State University Press, 1955; reprinted, 1985.

Wise, Stephen R. *Gate of Hell: Campaign for Charleston Harbor, 1863*. Columbia: University of South Carolina Press, 1994.

FAMILY PAPERS AND MANUSCRIPTS

Calendar of selected papers, 1861–1865, of Stephen Elliott (1830–1866) among the Elliott family papers, South Caroliniana Library, University of South Carolina.

Carter G. Woodson Papers, Manuscript Division, Library of Congress Transcription.

Charles Thomson Haskell family papers, 1819–April 1861. Located at the South Carolina Historical Society.

C.L. Burckmyer correspondence, 1863–1865. Located at the South Carolina Historical Society.

Daniel H. Hamilton Case Records, 1867–1870. Located at the South Carolina Historical Society.

John Grimball family papers, 1804–1893 (bulk 1858–1885). Located at the South Carolina Historical Society.

Letters of Stephen Elliott. Located at the South Caroliniana Library, University of South Carolina.

Pickens-Bonham Papers, Manuscript Division, Library of Congress.

Newspapers
Charleston Courier
Charleston Mercury
Cleveland Herald
Cleveland Plain Dealer
Columbia Guardian
Harper's Weekly
New Bedford Mercury
News and Courier
New York Herald
New York Times
Ohio State Journal
US News

INDEX

ABOUT THE AUTHOR

Pat Hendrix is an educator and cultural resources consultant, researching and writing on American history for public and private clients. He writes on topics as diverse as African pottery production in colonial Charleston; coal mining in West Virginia; cattle ranching in West Texas; the architectural history of Deadwood, South Dakota; and rice planting in colonial and antebellum South Carolina. His manuscripts include *Murder and Mayhem in the Holy City* and *Down and Dirty: Archaeology of the South Carolina Lowcountry*. He currently spends most of his time waiting for surf and worrying about the outcome of college football games.

Visit us at
www.historypress.net
....
This title is also available as an e-book